WE CAN'T CHANGE WHAT
WE DON'T KNOW

WE CAN'T CHANGE WHAT WE DON'T KNOW

HOW I STARTED TO THINK OF FOOD AS MEDICINE

KATHLYN CARNEY

NEW DEGREE PRESS

WE CAN'T CHANGE WHAT WE DON'T KNOW

How I Started to Think of Food as Medicine

ISBN   978-1-64137-342-5 *Paperback*

          978-1-64137-664-8 *Ebook*

This book is dedicated to my students for reminding me of the importance of listening and telling stories. Thank you for reigniting my passion for writing.

CONTENTS

"The rest is still unwritten"

—NATASHA BEDINGFIELD

THE WAY WE THINK ABOUT FOOD

When we go out to eat, we have so many options.

There are restaurants that tell us which options are vegan, vegetarian, keto, gluten-free, dairy-free, and nut-free.

We can go to restaurants that are farm to table and focused on serving locally grown foods. We can also eat out at places that only sell organic and high-quality fruits, vegetables, and meats.

However, with all of these new options comes scrutiny.

People see "vegan" or "organic" and think it is a "hippie restaurant" that "doesn't have *real* food."

When I posted a survey on Facebook and Instagram asking my followers what comes to mind when they hear the word "vegan," some responses were "expensive," "insufferable," "weird," and "annoying." This negative attitude about eating a certain way may be why many people don't consider how food directly impacts physical and mental health.

The majority of survey takers said they "sometimes" eat organic foods, and eighty-two percent stated it is important to avoid foods with added hormones.

People also said they would choose to eat organic or sustainable foods if prices were comparable to those of non-organic.

In addition, many of the respondents indicated that they do not think about the ingredients in their food or how their food is grown. Some of my followers stated that they do not eat Genetically Modified foods or foods with added pesticides. Lastly, only a handful of people who responded to my survey reported that they think about animal welfare or where their produce is grown.

While my respondents may not think about what is in their food or how it is grown, every single person who took the survey said they knew between **one and fifteen people** who has a food-related illness or allergy.

On top of that, every person who took the survey said they believe their diet impacts both their physical and mental health.

After reading what people had to say in the survey, I began to wonder where the disconnect lies.

Why do people believe diet impacts their physical and mental health but do not think about where their food comes from?

Why, if there are so many people with food allergies or food-related illnesses, do we think people who choose to eat the best quality foods are "annoying"?

I believe the disconnect occurs because people do not have time to research how food could be impacting their health and because there is a belief that eating healthy is expensive and time consuming.

The purpose of this book is to show you how I came to discover how diet has influenced my own health and the health of important people in my life.

I also offer insight on how to make healthy eating on a budget a reality.

I am going to break down all the research my friends, family, and I have done so you can use this information to get healthier and stop harnessing a negative view of eating a certain way.

HOW TO USE THIS BOOK

———

Whether you are looking to get healthy, dealing with a chronic illness, or are a friend of someone fighting an illness, there is information in this book to help you.

The book is broken up into three parts:

- Part 1 contains the introduction and additional chapters. In Part 1, you will learn why I am so passionate about using food as medicine instead of traditional medicine. You will also learn about two key parts of your body: the liver and the gut.

- Part 2 contains Chapters 4 to 10. In Part 2, you will read about why I decided to cut out foods like dairy, bread, corn, and eggs! You will read research from countless doctors that shows some foods we think of as healthy might not be good for us at all.

- Part 3 contains Chapters 11 to 17. In Part 3, you will get tangible tips and resources you can use to eliminate toxins and chemicals from your diet and home. You will also read my mom's success story and how she spent thirty years finding the cure for her mystery illnesses.

KEY TAKEAWAYS

If you are looking for immediate information, there are Key Takeaways listed at the end of Chapters 2 through 14. The Key Takeaways list contains the most important information in each chapter. In addition, Chapter 16 lists my favorite foods, brands, and products to keep in the home. You can look at my recommendations to make easy and informed decisions on what you want to buy.

AUTHOR RECOMMENDATION

If you want to get the most out of this book, I suggest you read it in order. Each chapter details my personal journey with food and includes insights from friends, family, and trusted researchers. I recommend that you read the entire book, so you truly understand that lifestyle changes take time and that there is no one cure to healing mystery illnesses.

You can decide how you use the suggestions and recommendations and how you interpret the stories and advice from some of the most inspiring women in my life.

PART 1

CAN FOOD BE USED AS MEDICINE?

INTRODUCTION

"Why are there craters on your face?"

Growing up with acne was extremely difficult. I was called names like "cake face" because of the amount of cover up that I had to use to hide my zits.

Yeah, not the best for the ego.

Little did many of the people who made these comments know that over the course of the last twelve years, I have seen dozens of dermatologists, estheticians, homeopathic practitioners, and traditional medicine doctors to try to cure my acne.

And while my skin has gotten significantly clearer since I was prescribed Accutane, I still have scars and skin damage.

I never wanted to have to take Accutane in the first place.

I did not want to have to sign pages and pages of documents stating that I understood all of the risks that came with taking the drug.

I did not want to have blood tests every month to make sure my organs were still functioning properly, especially since I am deathly afraid of needles and the mere sight of blood. At the start of every appointment at LabCorp, I would begin to feel faint as soon as I laid eyes on the purple rubber band that the technician would tie around my arm.

However, I went through this treatment process because I was tired of the creams, the antibiotics, the acupuncture, the supplements, the therapy...all of the methods I tried that did nothing to eliminate the bumps on my face.

I did it because not one person could tell me why my acne was so severe or why nothing cured it. And, quite honestly, I was tired of feeling bad about the way I looked or envious of my friends who didn't have to wear makeup on a daily basis.

It would take seven years after taking the drug to discover why I actually had cystic acne growing up.

My mom discovered a book by Anthony William, also known as the Medical Medium. She sent me his podcast called *Healing Eczema, Psoriasis & Acne* and a copy of the Medical Medium's

Medical Medium Liver Rescue: Answers to Eczema, Psoriasis, Diabetes, Strep, Acne, Gout, Bloating, Gallstones, Adrenal Stress, Fatigue, Fatty Liver, Weight Issues, SIBO & Autoimmune Disease.

She told me to listen and read because finally someone had answers to some of my questions.

And the answers weren't what I expected....

* * *

According to Statista, "The Centers for Medicare and Medicaid Services estimates that prescription drug expenditure in the United States came to some 333 billion U.S. dollars in 2017."[1]

And that price has only increased in the last two years.

---

1   Matej Mikulic, "Prescription Drug Expenditure U.S. 1960-2019," Statista (Statista 2019, August 9, 2019).

They also reported that "the United States is the country with the highest total drug spending and also with the highest per capita pharmaceuticals spending among developed countries."[2]

We have all heard about the opioid epidemic in the United States. The Centers for Disease Control and Prevention reported that "from 1999-2017, almost 400,000 people died from an overdose involving any opioid, including prescription and illicit opioids."[3]

At times it feels like the enormity of our health system sets us up to believe taking prescription drugs is the only way to cure an illness or ease our pain.

But is it?

* * *

Health is such a big, scary topic. Doctors go to school for decades to tell us what to do.

Why in the world should I write anything about health outcomes when I'm not a doctor? Seriously, I barely got by in

---

2   Matej Mikulic, "Prescription Drug Expenditure U.S. 1960-2019," Statista (Statista 2019, August 9, 2019).

3   "Understanding the Epidemic | Drug Overdose | CDC Injury Center," Centers for Disease Control and Prevention (Centers for Disease Control and Prevention, National Center for Injury Prevention and Control, December 19, 2018).

high school biology, so medical school was the furthest thing from my mind when choosing a career.

But something about my experience told me—compelled me, really—to start writing.

After deciding I wanted to write a book, I struggled to feel qualified. I am not an expert in anything, except for maybe embarrassing myself or getting into awkward situations. But once I reflected on the experiences I have had over the years, I decided I wanted to research and discover whether food can really cure illnesses that are typically prescribed antibiotics, chemotherapy, or other drug-focused treatments.

But it took others to convince me to actually share these findings.

I made the decision to write about this subject because I had been engaging in conversations with two of my friends and my mom about what we should be eating. My best friend from high school, Trish, was diagnosed with cancer in March 2018. My sorority sister, old roommate, and great friend, Alexandra, had been diagnosed with so many illnesses over the years and her health only continued to decline until she was practically bedridden and experiencing paralysis in her face. My mother also faced many different diagnoses over the years, from chronic fatigue and fibromyalgia to heavy metal toxicity to Candida.

My friends and my mom have all experienced rare illnesses that traditional doctors have only been able to help so much. Trish, Alexandra, and my mom were all prescribed many different medications while doctors tried to help. However, no doctor was ever able to tell my friends and my mother WHY they were suffering or HOW a twenty-three-year-old developed stage 4 cancer.

Even though I haven't been diagnosed with any serious illnesses, ever since I was eleven years old, I've struggled with acne. Doctors also have never been able to give me answers as to why I had chronic acne. Doctors said it was due to hormones and genes, but no one in my family experienced acne like I did.

* * *

As I previously mentioned, Alexandra had been fighting unknown illnesses since she was in middle school. She explained that she had been diagnosed with "Multiple Sclerosis, Lyme Disease, Fibromyalgia, Bell's Palsy, faulty genes, autoimmune disorders, Celiac Disease, Gastroparesis, Crohn's disease, C. Diff Infection, thyroid imbalances, and parasite infections."

When I was living with Alexandra, doctors were treating her for parasites, and she was taking a few different medications.

I later learned that over the years her symptoms ranged from "anxiety, depression, brain fog, numbness throughout the body, brain lesions/tumors, extreme fatigue, migraines, joint pain, body pain, blurred vision, vertigo, tinnitus, nausea, food allergies, chemical sensitivities, mold allergies, vomiting a couple times a day for years and severe stomach pains."

However, she dealt with all of these symptoms like a warrior. When I lived with her in college, she was studying neurophysiology and making the most out of her college career.

Yet there were still weeks when she would stay in bed with the lights off because she was feeling so sick.

Unfortunately, she reached a point a few years later where she was bedridden and had paralysis in her face. She could barely talk or walk and was in and out of hospitals with absolutely no hope. She was continuously being prescribed different medications for all of the various illnesses doctors thought she might have. No doctor was telling her anything definite, but they continued to prescribe her medications.

Luckily, during this time one of her father's friends, and eventually one of Alexandra's "soul sisters," recommended she read a book by Anthony William. The book Alexandra was given was *Medical Medium: Secrets Behind Chronic and Mystery Illness and How to Finally Heal*. After reading this book, she discovered she was suffering from an aggressive strain of the Ebstein-barr virus.

Alexandra was finally able to get to the root causes of her mystery illnesses.

She started to heal herself by changing her diet. She filled her body with fruits, vegetables, herbs, wild foods, and the right supplements. In addition, she took out certain foods that feed the virus, such as gluten, dairy, eggs, corn, soy, msg, and canola oil. And guess what—she started to feel like she had control of her health again.

When I talked to her about the change recently, she said, "I realized that I was starting to feel better because I was able to go to work, then go to Pilates, and make dinner when I got home. I was able to have a normal routine."

This routine is something Alexandra had been missing for almost a DECADE.

* * *

Alexandra's turnaround came full circle with myself, Trish, and my mother's journey when I ran into Alexandra at a Philadelphia Eagles game in September 2018. My mom had just sent me the book and a podcast by the Medical

Medium, and I was debating whether I wanted to take the time to read it.

As fate would have it, Alexandra looked amazing and had an abundance of energy.

I asked her, "How are you feeling?"

"Great," she responded.

This was the first time I had heard her give this answer and truly mean it.

She went on to explain all about her journey over the last year and how she believed changing her diet saved her life.

While I was not looking for anything to save my life, I was looking for something to help Trish.

* * *

In August, Trish finished her sixth round of chemotherapy. As I mentioned before, in March 2018, Trish was diagnosed with cancer. Her cancer is called a thymoma, which is a tumor caused by the autoimmune disease Myasthenia gravis.

The autoimmune disease is rare to begin with.

Developing a tumor is even more rare.

Developing a tumor at age twenty-three? Unheard of.

Doctors and specialists made the best decisions they could given the rarity of circumstance and advised Trish to get four to six rounds of chemotherapy to try to shrink the tumor before surgically removing it. Trish's tumor is located between her heart and her lungs—a less than ideal location to have surgery.

After her sixth round of chemotherapy, doctors informed her the tumor did not shrink enough to have the surgery.

They said the surgery was too risky, and, if she did have the surgery, her left lung would have to be removed.

Trish and I have been through it all together—from break-ups to high school dances to college visits to beach trips to basketball team drama.

A story that exemplifies our friendship is from our senior year of high school. We enrolled in a class together called "Conflict in the 21st Century."

Honestly, we only took the class because we heard you watched movies every day. Little did we know that every movie would be extremely graphic, and we would have to cover our eyes for half the films.

Our teacher would consistently make fun of us for being so squeamish but also for being inseparable. When one of us was absent, he would tease us and ask, "How are you going to get through the day without Churchill?" or "Carney?"

Even though he was joking, we really did rely on each other every single day. And even though time zones and thousands of miles have separated us since high school, we have still continued to rely on each other every day.

Considering I am so close to Trish, you can imagine how heartbreaking the news that chemotherapy was not successful was. Knowing how heartbroken I was, I could only imagine how my best friend felt.

Fortunately for every person who knows and loves Trish, she is a fighter.

In an update she posted on her GoFundMe page, she wrote "However, as a young twenty-three year old girl, I truly feel lucky that, for the most part, I have been able to go about my daily activities as "normal" Trish! As my friend Kathlyn mentioned in her original post, my goal was to finish my last academic semester on time and to continue into my final year of clinical rotations as planned. So far, I am proud to say that I have been able to accomplish all of that – something that certainly makes me happy and is a great distraction from all of this."[4]

She refused to be defeated by this diagnosis. She went on to not only finishing her rotations, but also to become A DOCTOR of PHARMACY.

Trish has shown so many people what it means to live life to the fullest and to be resilient. So, when she did not get the results that she wanted from her oncologist, she continued to seek out more opinions from doctors and specialists, and we searched for alternative options.

* * *

After hearing Alexandra's testimony, admittedly a little tipsy off a few too many Miller Lites at the Eagles' game, my mom and I decided to try following Anthony William's protocol. My mom had been experiencing some of the same symptoms as Alexandra, like fatigue, brain fog, and anxiety. She has always eaten healthy, but she made the commitment to truly follow his protocol after seeing how much it helped Alexandra.

---

4   Churchill, Trish. "Trish's Fight Against Thymoma." GoFundMe. GoFundMe, August 13, 2018.

Aside from Alexandra's testament to follow the advice of the Medical Medium, after I read the Acne chapter of his *Liver Rescue* book, I was convinced.

William's research suggests I have acne because, when I was born, my mom passed along the Streptococcus bacterium, or strep. When strep gets caught in your liver, it has to push out toxins through the skin. However, these toxins do not normally show up until puberty. As we all know, puberty is a time when a child's stable immune system boards a roller coaster and coasts through patterns of dips and turns, lowering its protection of some organs to focus on others.

When your immune system is lowered, you are also more susceptible to illnesses like bronchitis. Anthony William explained that the toxins from the antibiotics for illnesses like bronchitis also get stuck in the liver. And where do these toxins come out? Your skin.

And what do you know? I got bronchitis in sixth grade, around the exact same time I started to get acne.

Then, after reading *Liver Rescue*, I also discovered that the toxins from the antibiotics for pneumonia can get stuck in your liver, and eventually have to come out through the skin. And what did I have when I was two? You guessed it—pneumonia.

Suddenly, everything started to make sense.

Suddenly, I had some answers.

I have acne because there are toxins and bacteria stuck in my liver.

After having this ah-ha moment and feeling like it was fate that my mom had just discovered this book and sent it to me and that I ran into Alexandra at an Eagles game after not seeing her for almost two years, I felt a plethora of emotions, ranging from relief to anger.

I was relieved that I finally had an explanation as to why my skin was never like any of my friends'. But I was also angry that I went through so many appointments in which my esthetician would do excruciating extractions and laser treatments and that I had to go to junior prom embarrassed to wear my dress with cut outs because I had so many dry skin patches from the Accutane.

After going through all ~the feels~, I felt compelled to make the lifestyle changes the Medical Medium suggested—changes no one else had ever seriously suggested to me. He stated that dairy and eggs feed the toxins in your liver, so the only way the liver can start to heal itself is if you stop eating those foods.

If you know me, you know my diet consisted of quesadillas, cheese and crackers, chips and queso, ice cream, yogurt, grilled cheese and tomato soup—pretty much all things dairy.

Needless to say I was reluctant to make the change, but once I found yummy alternatives, it wasn't so terrible.

Then, I started to eliminate other foods he said did not support the liver, like gluten, pork, soy, canola oil, and corn.

The Medical Medium is also responsible for the viral celery juice trend. I've been trying that, too, and can honestly say it's not as bad as it sounds!

After about a month of doing this diet, I started to see changes in both my physical and mental health, and not just with my skin. I had more energy after work to exercise, go to graduate school class, or cook dinner. I also was feeling so much less anxious or stressed.

My mom was also seeing similar results. She had so much more energy and felt like she had control over her body again.

I distinctly remember sitting at my dining room table, *Liver Rescue* open, and telling Trish all of this new information.

"Can you believe that Anthony William offers insight as to why I have acne, and why you have an autoimmune disease?" I asked.

"Honestly, Kath, this is the exact opposite of everything that I have learned in Pharmacy school, but at this point, I'm willing to try anything."

She and her boyfriend, Steven, started reading *Liver Rescue* and a book called *Chris Beat Cancer: A Comprehensive Plan for Healing Naturally* by Chris Wark after hearing Alexandra's story and doing their own research. Trish and Steven decided to take the plunge with us and try this restrictive diet.

Finally, we all had a little more hope.

I had hope that my skin would improve and that my friends and family would start to feel better.

Trish had hope that there could be another option besides surgery.

My mom and Alexandra had hope that they would no longer receive countless diagnoses and prescriptions for illnesses that they may have never had.

Anthony William's books were how we got started on this journey.

After seeing what his dietary suggestions did for his followers and some of the people closest to me, I wanted to know more.

I wanted to know if other doctors and researchers were giving out similar information. I also wanted to know what other information is out there to help us live the healthiest lifestyle.

In this book, you'll hear stories and insights about:

- Two important parts of our body: the liver and the gut

- Foods that you might want to consider eliminating from your diet

- Supplements and foods to incorporate into your diet

- Products that you can use to reduce the amount of chemicals in your home

I do not want people to have to feel like their questions are unanswered or feel like they have to take a dangerous drug to feel good about themselves.

This book contains information from doctors and researchers and tells a little bit more about my health journey.

Keep reading to learn more about how specific dietary changes will have you living your healthiest life. You can only change once you know what to do.

CHAPTER 1

FOOD AS MEDICINE

———

Can food really be used as medicine?

Why can't I rely solely on modern medicine?

As a twenty-three-year-old with a journalism and psychology undergraduate degree and a master's degree in education, I have to admit that I do not know much about modern medicine.

My "Biology 101" course did not quite prepare me to write a book about what cancer patients should be doing to heal or medications people should avoid.

That is not my intention in writing this book.

However, the experiences detailed in my introduction have led me to believe food can be used as an additional layer of defense.

My mother also instilled in me that eating quality foods and living a healthy lifestyle can prevent illnesses and diseases. She taught me natural and homeopathic ways to deal with minor ailments like headaches, fevers, stomachaches, or colds.

Obviously, anytime I was really sick she would take me to the doctor and give me what the doctor prescribed.

However, aside from being a relatively ill baby and toddler, I only remember two times in my life that I needed to take antibiotics prescribed by a doctor.

I got Bronchitis when I was in fourth grade and the flu when I was in seventh grade.

Like I said before, I am not a doctor or a medical student, so I cannot say for certain that my good fortune is because of the foods that I ate and my active lifestyle. However, I do not think that they caused negative effects on my health!

On the other side of this, three extremely important people in my life who have been diagnosed with cancer did not have consistently healthy diets.

Two of those people were my grandparents, Norma and Ron, who are no longer with us. They both died from cancer.

My grandmother died of colon cancer, and my grandfather died of kidney cancer.

From what I remember, the majority of food my grandparents ate were processed. They did not make the choice to buy organic produce or grass-fed meat.

My grandmother kept an Italian household full of breads, pastas, meats, and cheeses.

When I would have sleepovers with my grandparents, I would have the Kid Cuisine TV dinners at night and pancakes in the morning after church. When my grandfather would take me out to eat, we would always get burgers and milkshakes. Needless to say, none of my memories of eating with my grandparents involved "healthy" foods.

I also remember when my grandmother learned that she had advanced colon cancer, my mother moved her and my grandfather into our house before she underwent life-threatening surgery.

My mom said my grandmother's body needed to be nourished. She wanted my grandmother to have the best chance of fighting her cancer and surviving surgery.

My grandmother did survive the surgery and lived a few weeks longer.

Unfortunately, the cancer was too aggressive and far along for a diet and lifestyle change to make a drastic difference. My grandmother was only sixty-eight when she died.

Even though I was only nine years old when she passed away, a seed was planted in my mind that a healthy diet was the key to living a long life.

Little did I know that I would show these beliefs thirteen years later when another important person in my life was diagnosed with an aggressive cancer.

When Trish was diagnosed with cancer, I was nowhere near as knowledgeable about healthy eating as I am now. However, I did believe she needed to be eating foods that would nourish her body and make it strong enough to fight cancer and survive chemotherapy.

Before her diagnosis, Trish's diet consisted of pizza, chicken fingers, Trix yogurt, and fruit.

She was the pickiest eater.

To give her some credit, she did start to incorporate Caesar salad and a few other healthier choices into her diet as she got older, but that was about it.

Throughout our decade long friendship, I made fun of her for eating so poorly. I would also tease her because there were only about five restaurants that we could go out to eat together in high school. This was because Trish knew she would like something on the menu.

However, I never could have imagined how much her selective diet might have impacted her health until we were forced to cross that bridge. Like I said before, Trish found out that she had cancer at age twenty-three.

One of the first things I did when Trish was diagnosed with a thymoma was create a "cancer fighting foods list." At first, the list consisted of what I could Google and find online.

My mom was also on board with pumping Trish with the best possible foods. Because I was living in Dallas and Trish was in Philadelphia, my mom would put together smoothie packs and bone broth soup to send her during the week. My mom and I already knew some of the healing benefits of bone broth and the nutritional value of many fruits. These packages were a small way we could help Trish add some nutrients to her picky diet.

During this time, Trish underwent six rounds of chemotherapy. As many of us know, chemotherapy kills cancer cells, but it also kills healthy cells. This was a risk we were all aware of when Trish started treatment, but it is what the doctors recommended to shrink her 7 cm x 7 cm x 13 cm tumor lodged between her heart and lung.

Trish and I have a lot in common, including our fear and dismay of going to the doctor, getting shots, or having anyone come near us with medical devices.

Luckily, Trish was able to overcome her fear and adapt. That is one of the many things I admire about her: she is able to adapt and deal with any situation.

She was able to adapt when she was told repeatedly the chemotherapy was unsuccessful and the tumor was not shrinking.

She was also able to handle the news that her tumor was essentially inoperable a few weeks later.

Trish adapted by looking for other options.

One of those options was changing her diet. Trish discovered *Chris Beat Cancer* and *Liver Rescue*, and these books became her bible for dietary decisions.

In the first few chapters of *Chris Beat Cancer*, author Chris Wark explained some of the inefficiencies of our health care system. There were three main points from his book, which I highly recommend reading if you or a loved one is diagnosed with cancer, that I took away.

The first point that he made was that the hospital did not offer him very nutritious food. He was offered foods like Jell-O and sloppy joes.[5] I am fortunate enough to have never had to stay overnight in a hospital—knock on wood—so I had no idea what kind of food they serve patients. I was shocked to find out that hospitals are not pumping their patients with fruits, vegetables, and foods to help them fight their illness. I am sure it has to do with budgets, but it is still unacceptable in my mind.

The second point that stuck with me was that in countries that consume fewer animal products and less processed food, there are lower cancer rates.[6] Many of the other books I have read have emphasized that countries that culturally have a more plant-based diet have lower cancer rates. One study by Dr. John McDougall that was done in Hawaii supported what Chris Wark reported. McDougall found that the older

5   Wark, Chris. "Into the Jungle." Essay. In Chris Beat Cancer, 1st ed., 7–11. Carlsbad, CA: HAY HOUSE, INC, 2018.
6   Wark, Chris. "Heroic Doses." Essay. In Chris Beat Cancer, 1st ed., 126–28. Carlsbad, CA: HAY HOUSE, INC, 2018.

Hawaiian patients ate more plant-based diets like "grains (like rice), fresh vegetables, beans, and fruit."[7] These patients were not facing the same chronic illnesses their children or grandchildren were experiencing. His research challenged the idea that illnesses are primarily genetic. Both of these findings made me start to believe that plant-based diets may be a key to preventing cancer or chronic illnesses.

Lastly, Chris Wark wrote that the third leading cause of death in the United States is death as a result of medical treatment. Yes, you read that right! Chris Wark went into further detail of what this statistic means specifically and what is classified as "death as a result of medical treatment."[8] However, I think this known statistic says so much about the measures we should take when we fall ill or to prevent needing medical care in the first place.

Chris Wark's reports only fueled my fire to discover whether food could truly be used as medicine and made me question if antibiotics were always the answer.

Anthony William's *Liver Rescue* also made me consider using food as medicine.

---

7   McDougall, John. "A Revelation: Your Health Is Not Determined by Heredity." Dr. McDougall's Health & Medical Center. John A. McDougall. Accessed October 9, 2019.

8   Wark, Chris. "Doctor's Orders." Essay. In Chris Beat Cancer, 1st ed., 43–47. Carlsbad, CA: HAY HOUSE, INC, 2018.

This notion really hit home for me while I was reading Chapter 23 of *Liver Rescue,* which is dedicated to acne. As I previously mentioned, Anthony William explained the cause of acne is Streptococcus in the liver. According to him, antibiotics feed strep and keep it in the liver.[9]

If you have suffered from acne, you know how it can be a never-ending process. Doctors prescribe you one medication or topical cream to try, and, when that doesn't work, they try another one. This phenomenon could explain why it is so difficult to cure chronic acne. The more antibiotics that we feed strep with, the stronger the strep gets, and the worse the acne seems.

In addition, Vincanne Adams and Dr. Michelle Perro wrote in *What's Making Our Children Sick? How Industrial Food Is Causing an Epidemic of Chronic Illness, and What Parents (and Doctors) Can Do About It* that research has shown antibiotics, not specifically the antibiotics used to treat acne, "create an unhealthy gut biome."[10]

---

9 William, Anthony. "Chapter 23 Acne." Essay. In Medical Medium Liver Rescue: Answers to Eczema, Psoriasis, Diabetes, Strep, Acne, Gout, Bloating, Gallstones, Adrenal Stress, Fatigue, Fatty Liver, Weight Issues, SIBO & Autoimmune Disease, 1st ed., 155–60. Carlsbad, CA: Hay House, Inc., 2018.

10 Perro, Michelle, and Vincanne Adams. "Food-Focused Medicine for a Pharmaceutical-Heavy World." Essay. In What's Making Our Children Sick?: How Industrial Food Is Causing an Epidemic of Chronic Illness, and What Parents (and Doctors) Can Do about It, 31. White River Junction, VT: Chelsea Green Publishing, 2017.

The authors go on to add that despite the medications we take and how medications impact our gut, we can control what we eat. What we eat "holds the greatest capacity to nourish us or, as the case may be, to harm us."[11]

This belief in the power of food is the philosophy I have developed.

I cannot control the antibiotics I have taken in the past or the antibiotics I may need in the future. However, I have full control of the food I put into my body to ensure I am as healthy as I can be.

After reading this book and seeing how food could be used as a line of defense, I was forced to consider the idea of food as medicine.

In this book, I will offer the wisdom I have taken from the following books: *Eat to Beat Disease: The New Science of How Your Body Can Heal Itself* by Dr. William Li, *Medical Medium Liver Rescue: Answers to Eczema, Psoriasis, Diabetes, Strep, Acne, Gout, Bloating, Gallstones, Adrenal Stress, Fatigue, Fatty Liver, Weight Issues, SIBO & Autoimmune Disease*

---

11 Perro, Michelle, and Vincanne Adams. "Food-Focused Medicine for a Pharmaceutical-Heavy World." Essay. In What's Making Our Children Sick?: How Industrial Food Is Causing an Epidemic of Chronic Illness, and What Parents (and Doctors) Can Do about It, 31. White River Junction, VT: Chelsea Green Publishing, 2017.

by Anthony William, *Eat Real to Heal: Using Food As Medicine to Reverse Chronic Diseases from Diabetes, Arthritis, Cancer and More* by Nicolette Richer, *Food: What the Heck Should I Eat?* by Dr. Mark Hyman, *What's Making Our Children Sick? How Industrial Food Is Causing an Epidemic of Chronic Illness, and What Parents (and Doctors) Can Do About It* by Dr. Michelle Perro and Vincanne Adams, *Chris Beat Cancer: A Comprehensive Plan for Healing Naturally* by Chris Wark, research done by Dr. John McDougall, and *Become Healthy or Extinct* by Darryl D'Souza.

CHAPTER 2

LOOKING AT YOUR WHOLE SELF AND YOUR MICROBIOME

Medical Anthropology: "the study of how health and illness are shaped, experienced, and understood in light of global, historical, and political forces"[12]

Vincanne Adams has made a career as a professor of medical anthropology.

How did she discover her passion?

---

12 "Medical Anthropology." Medical Anthropology | Department of Anthropology. Stanford University. Accessed October 9, 2019.

Her journey began when she was a PhD student. She learned about the influence pharmaceutical companies had on medical education.

It continued when she met alternative medicine practitioners while she was teaching at Princeton University who explained the lack of nutrition classes offered in medical school.

Her journey was also influenced by her research on Tibetan medicine.

Adams explained that Tibetan medicine starts with the idea that food is the first line of insult or defense to the body. She became extremely interested in the way Tibetan doctors view food.

After talking with Adams, I was also curious about Tibetan medicine and wanted to learn more.

I discovered that when Tibetan doctors evaluate a patient, they explore the patient's humoral constitution.

An article by Dr. Paolo Roberti di Sarsina, Luigi Ottaviani, and Joey Mella titled "Tibetan medicine: a unique heritage of person-centered medicine" explained that a person's humor is "determined by the diet and behavior of a child's mother during pregnancy."[13]

The three humors that are explored are wind, fire, and earth and water. When deciding which humor a person has, Tibetan doctors search for disparities in "body type, head shape, digestion, sleeping patterns, and emotional expressions."[14] In addition to looking at the mother's diet and behavior, the practitioners also look at the environment the patient lives in.

Doctors can look at these different factors and determine preventative measures for the diseases to which they predict a person could be susceptible.

Lastly, Tibetan medicine focuses on digestion when determining a diagnosis. The authors explained that "the way one digests gives valuable advice to imbalances in the body. Tibetan medicine considers an imbalance in any organ or part of the body (other than injury, etc.). For this reason each individualized medical treatment always incorporates herbal formulas, diet, behavior, and external

---

13 Sarsina, Paolo Roberti Di, Luigi Ottaviani, and Joey Mella. "Tibetan Medicine: a Unique Heritage of Person-Centered Medicine." *EPMA Journal* 2, no. 4 (2011): 385–89.

14 Ibid.

treatment that directly intend to bring balance and health to the digestive system."[15]

By incorporating all of these elements into a treatment plan, there is not one cure but multiple parts to a cure.

The way practitioners of Tibetan medicine and doctors in the United States view diagnosis differ in this way.

Seriously, the only American doctor I have ever seen investigate a patient's environment and factors outside of immediate symptoms was Dr. Greg House on the show *House*.

Adams and Perro wrote in their book that doctors in the U.S. are "taught a great deal about pharmaceutical solutions to health problems."[16]

This approach to medicine does not exactly take into account outside factors that could be impacting a person or alternative solutions to cure the problem.

---

15 Sarsina, Paolo Roberti Di, Luigi Ottaviani, and Joey Mella. "Tibetan Medicine: a Unique Heritage of Person-Centered Medicine." EPMA Journal 2, no. 4 (2011): 385–89.

16 Perro, Michelle, and Vincanne Adams. "Food-Focused Medicine for a Pharmaceutical-Heavy World." Essay. In What's Making Our Children Sick?: How Industrial Food Is Causing an Epidemic of Chronic Illness, and What Parents (and Doctors) Can Do about It, 23. White River Junction, VT: Chelsea Green Publishing, 2017.

Adams and Perro explain further that "pharmaceutical therapies targeting chronic, sometimes debilitating, disorders don't do much more than mask symptoms."[17]

So why do prescription drugs seem like doctors' go to treatment?

One reason might be because medical students are heavily influenced by pharmaceutical companies during their education. For example, Rijul Kshirsagar and Priscilla Vu reported in their article "The Pharmaceutical Industry's Role in U.S. Medical Education" that "forty to 100 percent of medical students report exposure to the pharmaceutical industry, with clinical students being more likely than preclinical students to report exposure."[18]

In addition to this exposure, Adams and Perro report that "[few] physicians today are taught much about the fact that many of the foods available to us *are not real foods* (or not *entirely* real foods). Nor are they systematically taught much of anything about what foods that have been grown with toxic ingredients or with added antibiotics or hormones are doing to our kids' bellies and bodies. This is not surprising.

---

17 Ibid.
18 Kshirsagar, Rijul, and Priscilla Vu. "The Pharmaceutical Industry's Role in U.S. Medical Education." in-Training. in-Training, April 5, 2016.

It is invisible partly because that information is not widely available, and what is available is often considered controversial. It is also invisible because we have not considered food a problem for long enough."[19]

Because of these less than ideal circumstances surrounding medical education, Adams wanted to learn more.

That is how she ended up partnering with Perro, who practices integrative medicine. Perro believes the contemporary food system that uses genetic engineering impacts children's health.

Adams was fascinated by what Perro was talking about. The two dived into research on the scientific literature available about the quality of food, soil, and pesticides.

So what did the two discover?

They learned how crucial the microbiome is on our health— and the impact that food has on our microbiome.

---

19 Perro, Michelle, and Vincanne Adams. "Food-Focused Medicine for a Pharmaceutical-Heavy World." Essay. In What's Making Our Children Sick?: How Industrial Food Is Causing an Epidemic of Chronic Illness, and What Parents (and Doctors) Can Do about It, 32. White River Junction, VT: Chelsea Green Publishing, 2017.

Dr. William Li, author of *Eat to Beat Disease,* explains that your microbiome is a collection of healthy bacteria in your body.[20]

Our bacteria, specifically in our gut, impacts so many functions, from our "immunity" to our "hormones."[21]

Li says our diet impacts our microbiome because "the way we eat can actually force the extinction of some gut bacteria, which can impact on the health of future generations."[22]

If having a lasting impact on your future children isn't terrifying enough, Li also states that "an unhealthy diet can by extension damage your angiogenesis defense, disrupt your stem cell function, make it harder for your body to protect its DNA, and compromise your immune system."[23]

As you can see, eating a healthy diet and keeping the bacteria in your gut healthy could help you—and your future children—avoid some serious issues.

---

20   Li, William W. "Chapter 3 Microbiome." Essay. In Eat to Beat Disease: the New Science of How the Body Can Heal Itself, 35–43. New York, NY: Grand Central Life & Style, 2019.

21   Ibid.

22   Li, William W. "Chapter 3 Microbiome." Essay. In Eat to Beat Disease: the New Science of How the Body Can Heal Itself, 47. New York, NY: Grand Central Life & Style, 2019.

23   Li, William W. "Chapter 3 Microbiome." Essay. In Eat to Beat Disease: the New Science of How the Body Can Heal Itself, 48. New York, NY: Grand Central Life & Style, 2019.

In addition, Adams and Perro found that the microbiome is impacted by the presence or absence of pesticides.[24]

Pesticides can affect health in different ways, depending on the person's age, genetics, how much they were exposed to, and other factors.

One of the main ways we ingest pesticides is by eating non-organic, genetically modified foods.

Many of these foods contain remnants of the weed killer called Roundup, which Adams said has been found to contribute to Hodgkin's lymphoma and impact liver and kidney function.

I'm sure you are wondering: why do we continue to eat foods that contain Roundup?

The answer is that there has been a huge pushback from the industries and communities that use Roundup, and the studies on Roundup have reported conflicting results. Many scientists still say Roundup is safe to use.

---

24 Perro, Michelle, and Vincanne Adams. "Leaky Gut: A Key to Understanding Pesticide Impact on Health" Essay. In What's Making Our Children Sick?: How Industrial Food Is Causing an Epidemic of Chronic Illness, and What Parents (and Doctors) Can Do about It, 81-92. White River Junction, VT: Chelsea Green Publishing, 2017.

Adams suggests that if you can cut out the number of pesticides in your food, you will eat healthier foods.

They also suggest that people stop looking for solutions to illness solely from antibiotics. Antibiotics can "create an unhealthy gut microbiome and that dysbiosis...can result from an imbalance of healthy versus unhealthy gut bacteria."[25]

According to Healthline, dysbiosis "occurs when the bacteria in your gastrointestinal (GI) tract — which includes your stomach and intestines — become unbalanced."[26]

This fact reinforces the importance of looking at the whole person when curing an illness and not just prescribing an antibiotic to treat it.

What can you do to keep your microbiome healthy?

- Adams explained you need to start paying more attention to the foods you eat.

---

25 Perro, Michelle, and Vincanne Adams. "Food-Focused Medicine for a Pharmaceutical-Heavy World." Essay. In What's Making Our Children Sick?: How Industrial Food Is Causing an Epidemic of Chronic Illness, and What Parents (and Doctors) Can Do about It, 32. White River Junction, VT: Chelsea Green Publishing, 2017.

26 "What Causes Dysbiosis and How Is It Treated?" Healthline. Accessed October 9, 2019.

- You should buy foods that are organic and have healthier ingredients.

- You should be sure to look at the ingredients in mass produced or packaged organic foods.

- Adams recommended that you purchase certified organic foods. She pointed out that, in the United States, we do not have to label GMOs and that labeling something as organic is not the same as labeling something non-GMO.

Adams ended our interview by stressing that your body's ability to use the food you eat depends on good quality nutrition and how well your body can break down the food and digest it.

If you feed your microbiome quality food, your microbiome will be healthy. She believes the microbiome is key to survival and health.

KEY TAKEAWAYS:
- Taking a look at your diet and environment can be crucial when you are trying to cure an illness.
- Do your best to eliminate pesticides in your diet and minimize antibiotics to protect your microbiome.
- Choose certified organic, non-GMO foods.

CHAPTER 3

THE LIVER IS YOUR BEST FRIEND

———

When I think of who my best friend is, quite a few names come to mind.

If I think about all of the qualities that my best friends share, the words loyal and supportive are at the forefront of my mind. All of my closest friends ensure I live my best life, whether that be by making me laugh or helping me weigh the pros and cons when I have to make a difficult decision.

Anthony William writes in *Liver Rescue* that "your liver is the best friend you've ever had. It performs over 2,000 critical functions that are undiscovered by medical research and science."[27]

Like my best friends, my liver supports me and helps me ensure that I live my best and healthiest life.

However, before I received a copy of Anthony William's *Medical Medium Liver Rescue: Answers to Eczema, Psoriasis, Diabetes, Strep, Acne, Gout, Bloating, Gallstones, Adrenal Stress, Fatigue, Fatty Liver, Weight Issues, SIBO & Autoimmune Disease,* I did not know that my liver was so vital to my health.

My previous knowledge of the liver included that is an organ, and we harm it when we binge drink a lot of alcohol.

William states that the liver's most critical functions are "processing fat and protecting the pancreas, glucose and glycogen storage, vitamin and mineral storage, disarming and detaining harmful minerals, screening and

---

27   William, Anthony. "Chapter 1 What Your Liver Does for You." Essay. In Medical Medium Liver Rescue: Answers to Eczema, Psoriasis, Diabetes, Strep, Acne, Gout, Bloating, Gallstones, Adrenal Stress, Fatigue, Fatty Liver, Weight Issues, SIBO & Autoimmune Disease, 1st ed., 5. Carlsbad, CA: Hay House, Inc., 2018.

filtering blood, and guarding you with its own personalized immune system."[28]

Clearly the liver does more than I ever realized.

Nicolette Richer simply explains in *Eat Real to Heal* that your liver "keeps your body clean, healthy, balanced, and detoxified." She also writes that the liver is "partly responsible for balancing hormones."[29]

Darry D'Souza explains how the liver is connected to your digestive system in *Become Healthy or Extinct*. He states that "although the liver separates out wastes that are carried by the blood to the kidneys where they are eliminated, certain toxins that come to the liver get passed into the bile that the liver produces. These toxic substances in the bile separate out and coat the liver ducts and the gall bladder chamber. Over time, they form stones that block the liver ducts and the gallbladder duct."[30]

---

28 William, Anthony. "Chapter 1 What Your Liver Does for You." Essay. In Medical Medium Liver Rescue: Answers to Eczema, Psoriasis, Diabetes, Strep, Acne, Gout, Bloating, Gallstones, Adrenal Stress, Fatigue, Fatty Liver, Weight Issues, SIBO & Autoimmune Disease, 1st ed., 8. Carlsbad, CA: Hay House, Inc., 2018.

29 Richer, Nicolette. "Detoxification." Essay. In Eat Real to Heal: Using Food as Medicine to Reverse Chronic Diseases from Diabetes, Arthritis to Cancer and More, 112–13. Coral Gables, FL: Mango, 2018.

30 D'Souza, Darryl. "The Liver." Essay. In *Become Healthy or Extinct!*, 6th ed., 33, 2019.

As you can see, it is crucial to make sure your liver is working properly and keeping your liver and gallbladder ducts clear.

And while our liver may be our "best friend" because it has to keep our body clean and carry out wastes, it is currently in danger due to "the toxins we are exposed to in everyday life."[31] Anthony William explains it is in danger because "our livers bear the brunt of the clean up job."[32]

Most people understand that we are exposed to toxins in the air through gas emission or from chemicals in drinking water.

However, many people do not understand the toxins, pesticides, and chemicals that come from the food that we eat. It is not commonly known how the foods that we put in our bodies impact our liver's ability to perform all of the functions that the authors above discussed.

Throughout this book, I am going to discuss foods that Anthony William and other doctors have advised people

---

31 William, Anthony. "Chapter 1 What Your Liver Does for You." Essay. In Medical Medium Liver Rescue: Answers to Eczema, Psoriasis, Diabetes, Strep, Acne, Gout, Bloating, Gallstones, Adrenal Stress, Fatigue, Fatty Liver, Weight Issues, SIBO & Autoimmune Disease, 1st ed., 6. Carlsbad, CA: Hay House, Inc., 2018.

32 Ibid.

to cut out because of the effect they have on the liver and the microbiome we previously mentioned.

Along with foods to avoid, the American Liver Foundation published "13 Ways to a Healthy Liver."[33]

KEY TAKEAWAYS FROM THE ARTICLE:

- Exercise regularly
- Use alcohol responsibly
- Don't share personal hygiene items
- Practice safe sex
- Wash your hands

Taking the time to exercise and practice these healthy habits will support your liver's ability to function.

---

33   "Healthy Liver - 13 Tips on How to Have a Healthy Liver." American Liver Foundation, January 7, 2019.

PART 2

WHAT SHOULD WE EAT?

CHAPTER 4

NO PROCESSED FOODS

—

"What? You only have water to drink?"

I heard this question time and time again when friends would come to my house for the first time growing up.

My response would always be an awkward "Uh...yeah my mom doesn't let us keep soda in the house."

Growing up, we were always known as the "healthy family" with "no good snacks." My mom always bought organic food, and we never had soda or sports drinks in the house. I definitely always felt self-conscious about not having Doritos or Gushers in the pantry when friends came over.

And don't even get me started about school lunches.

My mom would pack me a turkey and cheese sandwich on wheat bread, which at least made me seem normal to most kids. No one had to know that the turkey and cheese were organic. However, no one ever wanted to trade my apple slices or yogurt for their mainstream treats.

Explaining the research on processed foods may seem obvious.

Most of us understand that eating fast food is not optimal for our health and that eating a piece of fruit is definitely a better choice than eating a soft chocolate chip cookie. However, if this seems like common sense, why do we continue to hit up our favorite drive-through or binge eat an entire bag of Cheetos?

I have definitely been culpable for choosing junk food over a healthy snack.

My guilty pleasure growing up was always M&M's and Goldfish. Fortunately for my figure, my mom only let me have that delicious—and somewhat peculiar—combination every once in a while, or when I actually went to the grocery store with her and sneaked it in the cart.

I also had my dad, who would indulge me when I requested an extra cheese pizza or a cheeseburger at the local diner. While my dad has also supported healthy eating and a well-balanced lifestyle, he also always said I was "too thin" and needed to eat more.

I can thank my father for my healthy body image growing up.

Eventually, I discovered my mom never let me buy the "normal" snacks because many of these treats are heavily processed. Processed foods contain harmful additives, preservatives, and flavors.

Darry D'Souza explained these additives have almost no nutrition. He also noted that they destroy the good bacteria in the intestines.[34]

I did not know all of this growing up, but my mom sure did.

William Li reported that we should be taking a "low glycemic index approach" to our diet. He explains that we should minimize or avoid "sugary, processed foods containing little to no fiber that can cause blood sugar to spike, such as sugar sweetened-beverages and many packaged snack foods."[35]

---

34 D'Souza, Darryl. "Causes of Chronic Illness and Disease" Essay. In *Become Healthy or Extinct!*, 6th ed., 24, 2019.

35 Li, William W. "Chapter 7 (Re)generate Your Health" Essay. In *Eat to Beat Disease: the New Science of How the Body Can Heal Itself,* 149. New York, NY: Grand Central Life & Style, 2019.

So maybe it was really for the best that we did not have soda in our house growing up!

However, because I never had any "normal" snacks or drinks growing up, I always thought my mom was the weird or the crazy one. So, when I first got my driver's license in high school, I rebelled.

There was a Wawa near my high school in Delaware, and I would go there after school and get whatever snack I wanted. My favorites were White Cheddar Cheez-Its and Brown Sugar Cinnamon Pop-Tarts.

Luckily, I was a three-sport athlete, so the changes in my diet did not seem to show on the outside.

As I moved on from high school to college, my eating habits continued to be more and more unhealthy and go against all of the habits my parents tried to teach me. I drunk-ate McDonald's and Taco Bell with my friends weekly, and I survived on quesadillas made by my sorority's amazing chef, Marco.

I did not begin to notice how my change in diet affected me until my junior year. I had gained almost twenty-five pounds since the beginning of my freshman year, and I was constantly getting sick. Any time someone in my house—which was the home to sixty-seven girls—had a cold or pink eye, I always got it, too.

I started to realize my unhealthy habits were really starting to take a toll on my body and immune system. However, I was too busy working, studying, and admittedly partying to do anything about it. It was easier to eat the unhealthy buffet style meals provided by my sorority or to go to the drive-through during late night study sessions than to grocery shop or make a salad. I kept telling myself that as soon as I graduated, I would be healthy again.

When I moved to Dallas after graduating from the University of Maryland, I started to be health-focused. I shopped at Whole Foods and Trader Joe's and forced myself to start meal prepping and cooking.

It's honestly hilarious because the only "meals" I knew how to cook at age twenty-one were eggs, grilled cheese, and mac and cheese. Luckily, my roommate Jason was older, wiser, and knew how to cook. He definitely helped me figure out how to meal prep.

Even though I was making better choices, I was not seeing much of a change. I was only losing about a pound a month, and I was experiencing exhaustion and getting consistent colds. I tried to blame my symptoms on the long hours that

I worked at my school and because I was constantly surrounded by sniffling teenagers.

Finally, in the summer after my first year of teaching in Dallas, I knew it was time to make a more serious lifestyle change.

As soon as I made this commitment, I contacted my alternative health practitioner that I saw in high school. She recommended that I begin taking some supplements and engaging in Neuro Emotional Technique (NET).

NET is a "psycho-emotional therapy based on the physiological foundations of stress-related responses."[36] And, as many people have been told, stress is not good if you are fighting an illness.

Innovative Medicine's website explains that "NET's aim is not to cure the patient; rather, the therapy can be used comprehensively with other medical therapies to remove psycho emotional blocks that may aid in the ability of the body to repair itself naturally."[37]

I started receiving NET when I was in high school because it was thought to be one of the causes of my acne.

---

36 "Neuro Emotional Technique (NET)." Innovative Medicine.
      Accessed October 10, 2019.
37 Ibid.

However, during this summer in Dallas, I needed it because I was under immense stress. I was taking master's classes, starting a summer fellowship, in an emotionally draining relationship, processing that my best friend was getting chemotherapy and had just finished up teaching 150 seventh graders.

To say I had some "psycho emotional blocks" to remove would be an understatement.

While I was receiving NET, I also started to cook every meal at home and began training for a half marathon with my friend Rachel. I thought that by making all of these changes, I would start to see results.

However, that was not the case.

Throughout the whole summer, I only lost about five pounds. I started to feel better physically, but I was still experiencing some exhaustion and anxiety. It was extremely discouraging that I could be so dedicated to my health and not see significant results.

Luckily, my mom kept exploring other options with me.

As previously mentioned, my mom showed me the diet that the Medical Medium, Anthony William, suggested. His diet instructed you to cut out dairy, pork, eggs, canola oil, corn, soy, processed sugars, farm-raised fish, and a few other foods. I was intimidated to begin to cut out these foods, especially because eggs were a standard part of my diet.

In addition, starting this diet meant I had to give up almost all of my go-to frozen meals I would bring to school or make when I got home late from class. It meant I really had to cut out almost every kind of processed food.

But, this time, I was ready to give up convenience and make a more drastic change.

I was ready to stop feeling tired, anxious, and honestly unsatisfied with my appearance.

Astonishingly enough, within three months of making serious dietary changes, I lost almost fifteen pounds.

I went down an entire pant size.

I continued to work with my alternative health practitioner for advice on supplements and to continue NET.

Adams and Perro wrote an entire chapter on how cutting out genetically modified foods can improve mental health. I definitely was starting to see some of the impact that it had on my own happiness and energy level. By January, I felt like a completely different person.

I had more energy than ever, and I was able to take on two rewarding challenges: writing this book and dating.

I honestly had never formally dated before. Every previous boyfriend I had I was friends with first, so I had no idea how to even act on a first date.

I thought it was weird that a guy opened the car door for me when he picked me up—that's how clueless I was.

And even though I was feeling much more confident in my appearance, I was now worried about how guys would react to my dietary and lifestyle changes.

Lucky for me, it did not end up being a deal breaker.

I met someone in Dallas who embraced all of the research I did to find an effective diet and how health-focused I became. Luke respected my story and why I was so passionate to eat foods that were "diet compliant."

I will never forget when I brought him to meet Trish for the first time. Trish started talking about how we were trying to stick to diet compliant foods while she was visiting me in Dallas. We were explaining how it was hard not to take her to the greasy taco place or the pizzeria down the street while she was on vacation.

Luke just smiled and acted like it was totally normal that we had eaten salads for dinner before meeting up with him for drinks at a holiday pop-up bar.

He kept the positive attitude with every text that I sent him about a new food I wanted to eliminate from my diet or a recipe that I wanted to try.

Luke made me feel at ease about cutting more and more foods out of my diet and becoming a healthier person. Along with embracing my dietary restrictions, he helped me discover how to use my Apple Watch to meet daily exercise goals and get more sleep.

I would also like to think I helped him become a healthier person—I mean, he did start drinking celery juice after I forced him to try mine countless mornings.

During the months I made serious lifestyle changes and started dating Luke, I learned that instead of being afraid to share my health journey, I could find someone who would embrace it.

I also learned this by watching my friend Maria's boyfriend, Tim, completely embrace her vegan lifestyle. When I was out with him in Washington, DC, he commented that he made a reservation at a vegan restaurant for their one-year anniversary, even though he is not a vegan.

If that isn't love, I'm not sure what is.

If you are worried about the stigma that comes with being healthy or vegan when you are dating, just know there are people who will still like you when the only things you can order on the menu are salad or a plain baked potato, instead of processed and fried foods.

In my previous chapter, I discussed John McDougall's research in Hawaii. He discovered something very interesting that relates directly to what I've said about processed foods.

He examined the difference between his older patients and his younger patients. He noticed that his older patients followed the diet of their ancestors, sticking to mainly plant foods grown on the island. However, the younger patients ate more animal foods and processed foods.

He found that the older generation was not getting diagnosed with the chronic illnesses that the younger generation was. This negates the theory that the majority of illnesses are hereditary.[38]

---

38 McDougall, John. "A Revelation: Your Health Is Not Determined by Heredity." Dr. McDougall's Health & Medical Center. John A.

McDougall's research is just another example that shows how we can prevent or heal chronic illnesses with FOOD!

But what is in processed foods that make them almost as dangerous as having "bad" genes?

An article written by Cara Rosenbloom for The Washington Post indicated that the biggest danger lies within ultra-processed foods. Foods considered to be ultra-processed include: "candy, instant soups, ice cream, breakfast cereals, soda and hot dogs."[39]

Rosenbloom reported that "ultra-processed foods are high in sugar, fat and salt, and lack fiber, vitamins and minerals."[40] Due to the high fat and low nutrients, "people who consume more ultra-processed foods have a greater risk of obesity, hypertension and high blood sugar levels, which can lead to heart disease and diabetes."[41]

It's funny—or really not that funny—because my seventh grade students also joked about how the foods that they ate

---

McDougall. Accessed October 9, 2019.

39 Rosenbloom, Cara. "Not All Processed Foods Are Bad for You. How They're Made Matters." The Washington Post. WP Company, February 9, 2017.

40 Ibid.

41 Ibid.

like Takis and pizza were going to give them diabetes, but they might have been onto something.

An article by the Academy of Nutrition and Dietetics and reviewed by Taylor Wolfram indicated that the two biggest ingredients that you need to look out for are added sugar and sodium.[42]

The article indicated that if "the first two or three ingredients" include "sugar, maltose, brown sugar, corn syrup, cane sugar, honey and fruit juice concentrate," you might want to make a different choice.[43]

In regard to salt, the article stated we should choose foods with labels that say "no salt added, low-sodium or reduced-sodium."[44]

As I have continued to do my research, I've realized more and more foods I should include in my diet, not just foods I should remove. However, I think it is important for us to realize that even though processed food is convenient—and admittedly delicious—it is not worth it if you are facing consequences like I was, and it is

42 Wolfram, Taylor. "Processed Foods Whats OK and What to Avoid." EatRight . Academy of Nutrition and Dietetics , February 11, 2019.
43 Ibid.
44 Ibid.

definitely not worth it if you are facing worse consequences, like cancer.

Next time you are deciding between going to a drive-through or making a smoothie for the road, maybe throw all of your fruits and some spinach in your freezer in the blender and call it a day!

KEY TAKEAWAYS:

- Cut down on the number of processed foods you are buying.
- Look for the amount of sugar and sodium that are added to your processed foods.

CHAPTER 5

YES FRUITS AND VEGETABLES

———

"No."

"No" was the most common answer to the question "Do you actively think about what ingredients are in your food or how your food was grown/raised?" on the survey that I posed on my social media accounts.

After reviewing the answers that forty-four of my Facebook or Instagram friends graciously gave, I realized that my chapter about fruits and vegetables had to discuss the importance of eating organic and choosing foods that have not been genetically modified.

I also understood I needed to talk about how to make eating fruits and vegetables easy and affordable.

Many of the survey respondents that did not respond with a mere "no" indicated that a huge reason they do not choose to eat organic is because of the price.

My hope is that this chapter shows you why it is important to choose fruits and vegetables that will fuel your body on a budget.

As I mentioned, I've always chosen organic fruits and vegetables because that is what I grew up eating. I wasn't really sure why organic was better for me; I just knew that's what my mom said, and I stuck with it.

However, I would say it was difficult for me to consistently buy fresh fruits and vegetables when I was cooking and meal planning for one person. I would constantly throw out apples that had bruised or carrots that stayed in my fridge for much longer than I anticipated.

My biggest solution to this problem was utilizing a wonderful invention: the freezer.

I started to buy all of my fruits (except for apples, bananas, limes, and lemons) frozen, and consistently bought frozen riced cauliflower, spinach, broccoli, and peppers, which made it so much easier to reduce waste.

An article by Dr. Andrew Weil titled "Are Frozen Vegetables Healthy?" explained that frozen fruits and vegetables can have more nutritional value than fresh produce in some cases. "[They] usually are picked when they're ripe, and then blanched in hot water to kill bacteria and stop enzyme activity that can spoil food. Then they're flash frozen, which tends to preserve nutrients."[45]

In addition, if fresh produce was starting to go bad, like bananas or sweet potatoes, I would cut them up and add them to veggies in the freezer.

After I started to be less wasteful, I also wanted to know how I could continue to spend less.

In Dr. Mark Hyman's book, *Food: What the Heck Should I Eat?*, he included the Environmental Working Group's list, "The Dirty Dozen."[46]

He recommended that you buy all of the vegetables on the "Dirty Dozen" list organic.

---

45 Weil, Andrew. "Are Frozen Vegetables Healthy? - Ask Dr. Weil." DrWeil, December 3, 2016.
46 Hyman, Mark. "Vegetables." Essay. In Food: What the Heck Should I Eat?, 120. New York, NY: Little Brown & Co, 2018.

I also looked up the Environmental Working Group's "Clean Fifteen" list. This list contains the fruits and vegetables that you do not always need to buy organic because there is a smaller chance that they have absorbed dangerous chemicals.

Below are what are considered the Clean Fifteen and the Dirty Dozen:

THE "CLEAN FIFTEEN":[47]

1. Avocados
2. Sweet corn
3. Pineapples
4. Sweet peas (frozen)
5. Onions
6. Papayas
7. Eggplants
8. Asparagus
9. Kiwis
10. Cabbages
11. Cauliflower
12. Cantaloupes
13. Broccoli
14. Mushrooms
15. Honeydew melons

---

47 "Clean Fifteen™ Conventional Produce with the Least Pesticides." EWG's 2019 Shopper's Guide to Pesticides in Produce | Clean Fifteen. Environmental Working Group, 2019.

THE "DIRTY DOZEN":[48]

1. Strawberries
2. Spinach
3. Kale
4. Nectarines
5. Apples
6. Grapes
7. Peaches
8. Cherries
9. Pears
10. Tomatoes
11. Celery
12. Potatoes

This list can help you make smarter choices when deciding whether you want to splurge or if you would rather go with the cheaper option.

To me, these lists make a lot of sense. The majority of the foods listed in the "Dirty Dozen" are foods of which you eat the skin. The only item on the "Dirty Dozen" I had to be more conscious about buying organic was potatoes. I usually peel the skin off, so it was hard for me to remember to choose organic.

---

48 "Dirty Dozen™ Fruits and Vegetables with the Most Pesticides." EWG's 2019 Shopper's Guide to Pesticides in Produce | Dirty Dozen. Environmental Working Group, 2019.

However, my mom later informed me that you are supposed to keep the skin on potatoes to get added nutrients. So I guess it really does make sense!

For produce that is not included on this list, I would go with the rule that if you are not going to peel the skin or outer shell off, choose organic. It is the best way to ensure that you are not consuming harmful chemicals that remained on the produce after being picked.

Many of the survey respondents indicated they consider pesticides when they are buying produce. The "Dirty Dozen" and the "Clean Fifteen" are based on how likely the fruits and vegetables are to be exposed to pesticides. Using this list is one way people who do not want added pesticides on their food can also be more cost efficient.

Lastly, if you have to buy an item on the "Dirty Dozen" from the regular produce section, you can decrease your exposure to pesticides by washing your produce well. The way that my mom told me to clean my produce is by soaking it in baking soda. Choosing baking soda to clean your produce is both easy and cheap. All you need is a bowl, water, and baking soda. By cleaning your produce well, you are doing your best to protect your microbiome from pesticides.

I also read in Darryl D'Souza's book *Become Healthy or Extinct* that it helps to wash fruits and vegetables that you are going to eat the skin with "a scrubbing action under running tap water."[49]

He explains that this action "will dislodge natural dirt and germs on them."[50]

After that, D'Souza suggests "wiping them off firmly with a clean cloth" to "remove traces of pesticide."[51] Wiping is just another step to take to be sure you aren't harming your gut by eating foods we believe are healthy.

KEY TAKEAWAYS:

- Buy more organic, frozen produce.
- Use the "Dirty Dozen" and the "Clean Fifteen" to help you make cost effective decisions.
- Clean your produce before you eat it.

---

49 D'Souza, Darryl. "Blending" Essay. In *Become Healthy or Extinct!*, 6th ed., 88, 2019.

50 Ibid.

51 D'Souza, Darryl. "Blending" Essay. In *Become Healthy or Extinct!*, 6th ed., 88, 2019.

CHAPTER 6

YES ORGANIC FOOD

—

"Is it organic?"

Those three simple words constantly come out of mother's mouth.

She would ask this question at every restaurant we went to growing up and at every family holiday party.

As I got older and started to love trying new restaurants, my mom would consistently ask me if the restaurant served organic food before agreeing to try it with me.

Judging by some confused servers and family members' responses to her question, I do not think many people really know what it means to eat organic food.

An article on Unlock Food called "Understanding Organic Foods" explained that the main difference between organic and nonorganic is how the food is grown.

Organic foods are "produced without synthetic (human-made) pesticides, herbicides and fertilizers, [genetically] modified organisms (GMOs), [antibiotics] or growth hormones, and [Irradiation] or ionizing radiation (a way to preserve food with radiation energy)."[52]

When you choose to eat organic, you give your body a break from having to break down and digest all of the chemicals on or in your produce or meat.

Chris Wark included this tip in *Chris Beat Cancer:* "organic produce will have a 5-digit SKU [stock keeping number] starting with 9. GMO produce typically has a 5-digit SKU starting with 8, sometimes shortened to just 4 digits."[53]

You can check to make sure your produce is actually organic by looking at the SKU number.

52 "Understanding Organic Foods." Unlock Food. Dietitians of Canada, December 3, 2018.

53 Wark, Chris. "Take Out the Trash" Essay. In Chris Beat Cancer, 1st ed., 166. Carlsbad, CA: HAY HOUSE, INC, 2018.

As the years went on, my mother's list of restaurants she could eat at got shorter and shorter, and the list of food we would bring to family events got longer and longer.

And, let me tell you, it is extremely difficult to find restaurants that serve organic, locally grown cuisine.

When I was in college, we had two restaurants in Wilmington that we could go out to eat, and two restaurants in the DC area that we frequented. My friends would always joke that I only took my parents to the same restaurants each time they came down for a visit.

They definitely were not complaining, though, as all of the restaurants served impeccable dishes ranging from coconut tofu bites to edamame three ways.

In addition, I knew it was better to keep my mom happy than to have her get up and leave a restaurant because there was "nothing that she could eat."

Yes, that has happened multiple times in my life.

I will never forget the time my dad and I thought that we found a great farm to table restaurant to take my mom for her birthday in Wilmington. She sat down at the table, took a look at the menu and said, "Hopefully the chef can modify the salmon so that I can eat here."

My dad and I looked at each other and knew this meal was not going to end well.

When the waiter came to the table, my mom told him that she was gluten and dairy-free and wondered if the chef could take a dairy item off of the salmon. The waiter looked at her, frightened, and said she would go check with the chef.

The waiter slowly made her way back to the table with a fearful look on her face. She stated that the chef did not make modifications to the food.

My mom looked at her, looked at us, and stated, "Okay well there is nothing I can eat here."

And that was that.

We got up and went to Whole Foods to buy something to cook for her at home.

As you can imagine, I am by now immune to listening to my mom grill a young waiter—who probably has never wondered where his or her food was grown or if it was organic—and then claim that she was sorry, but there was nothing she could eat.

My personal favorites are the waiters who do not want to lose business and try and recommend the house salad. My mom would look at them straight in the eye and say, "That is not what I want."

She's kind of a boss.

And I agree with her—I mean who wants to pay to eat out to only get a salad with raw tomatoes, cucumbers, and onions?

I used to be mortified during these conversations. I would also feel embarrassed when our family would be invited out to eat, and we would have to decline because the restaurant did not have organic food or gluten-free options.

However, this situation started to change as I began to get to know people my age with dietary restrictions and embark on doing some of my own research.

Admittedly, I feel guilty about the embarrassment I felt when eating out with my mom. I feel terrible about how many times my mom has said, "Don't give me that look," or, "It's not my fault I don't want to be sick for the next few days."

Eating out has definitely gotten a lot easier now that we are on a similar page.

Nicolette Richer, the founder of the Richer Health Retreat Centre, stated the importance of eating organic. She wrote in her book *Eat Real to Heal* that "It's REALLY important. All caps. Non-negotiable."[54]

She explains that if you have an illness or if you are trying to be healthy, you want toxins to exit your body, not be brought in by food sprayed with pesticides.

I think changing our minds on what is truly "good" for us is imperative if we are going to use food as medicine.

In their book *What's Making Our Children Sick? How Industrial Food Is Causing an Epidemic of Chronic Illness, and What Parents (and Doctors) Can Do About It,* Perro and Adams address the confusion that people have regarding what truly is healthy.

The authors wrote, "Few physicians today are taught much about the fact that many of the foods available to us *are not real foods* (or not *entirely* real foods). Nor are they systematically taught much of anything about what foods have been grown with toxic ingredients or with added antibiotics and

---

54 Richer, Nicolette. "Frequently Asked Questions about Food and Disease." Essay. In Eat Real to Heal: Using Food as Medicine to Reverse Chronic Diseases from Diabetes, Arthritis to Cancer and More, 48-49. Coral Gables, FL: Mango, 2018.

hormones are doing to our kids' bellies and bodies. This is not surprising. It is invisible partly because that information is not widely available, and what is available is often considered controversial. It is also invisible because we have not considered food a problem for long enough."[55]

I think this paragraph is extremely relatable because a lot of the push back I get when I talk about my diet are comments like "Well, my grandmother ate this way her whole life and she is ninety and still living" or "The FDA would not approve foods we could not consume."

At first, I had no idea how to respond to these comments, because they are valid.

However, I think Perro and Adams sum it up perfectly: there is not enough information, and there is not enough information that is available to the average person.

Let's face it—if I did not know people who were facing chronic illnesses or cancers, I probably would not have gone looking for some of the information that is out there.

55 Perro, Michelle, and Vincanne Adams. "Food-Focused Medicine for a Pharmaceutical-Heavy World." Essay. In What's Making Our Children Sick?: How Industrial Food Is Causing an Epidemic of Chronic Illness, and What Parents (and Doctors) Can Do about It, 32. White River Junction, VT: Chelsea Green Publishing, 2017.

What I can say to skeptics is that I used to be one.

I used to challenge what my mother told me about food because no one else seemed to have eaten as restrictive of a diet as she did. I used to say, "Why do other kids' moms eat ice cream with them, but you don't?"

But now that I have seen the impact the food can have on people, either helping them or harming them, I think it is critical we examine the foods we are putting in our bodies.

Sorry for doubting you, mom—again.

Perro and Adams admitted that not all people "get sick from eating unhealthy foods at the same rate" and that the foods with pesticides, hormones, and added ingredients may be "doing damage to their guts and other organs (especially the liver) without realizing it."[56]

Just because a person doesn't develop acne, an autoimmune disease, or cancer, doesn't mean their organs are working perfectly.

---

56   Perro, Michelle, and Vincanne Adams. "The Family Eating Modern Industrial Foods: Almost Everyone Is Sick." Essay. In *What's Making Our Children Sick?: How Industrial Food Is Causing an Epidemic of Chronic Illness, and What Parents (and Doctors) Can Do about It*, 57. White River Junction, VT: Chelsea Green Publishing, 2017.

Finally, Perro includes a lot of case studies in the book that have me convinced we need to be more food-focused if all of our doctors are not going to be.

After describing a few patients that Perro had, the authors wrote that a parent of these patients felt "transitioning to organic and cutting out all GM foods was the big step that changed everything for all of them."[57]

Even though Adams and Perro were only discussing a few patients in one family, it could help you if you are suffering from some of the same symptoms their patients were. The children experienced a variety of issues like headaches, allergic reactions, and upset stomachs.

Our bodies were not built to process chemicals and genetically modified foods.

In an interview I had with Adams, she explained that your microbiome is impacted by the presence or absence of pesticides. Pesticides can affect health in different ways, depending on age, genetics, and how much you were exposed to.

---

57   Perro, Michelle, and Vincanne Adams. "The Family Eating Modern Industrial Foods: Almost Everyone Is Sick." Essay. In *What's Making Our Children Sick?: How Industrial Food Is Causing an Epidemic of Chronic Illness, and What Parents (and Doctors) Can Do about It*, 52-53. White River Junction, VT: Chelsea Green Publishing, 2017.

She also added that if you can cut out the number of pesticides in your food, you will be eating healthier foods.

It only makes sense that people are healthier if they pay attention to organic labels and use healthier ingredients in meals to start with.

One of the chemicals that we need to be aware of is Roundup. Roundup is a weed killer. Adams explained to me that, in the 1990s, people started to grow plants that had been genetically modified to resist Roundup.

However, even though the plants survive when Roundup is sprayed, that does not mean humans are supposed to eat foods that have been exposed to the chemical. Adams informed me that Roundup has been found to contribute to Hodgkin's lymphoma, poor liver function, and compromised kidney health.

In my previous chapter, I discussed the produce you should definitely buy organic. Many of the authors, researchers, and my mother agree buying organic produce is a huge step to take in eliminating toxins from our bodies and starting to heal!

Like my mother, I also now try to choose restaurants that are farm to table, vegan, or accommodate food allergies.

I even took my friends to a vegan restaurant in Philadelphia for my twenty-fourth birthday!

It's only a little terrifying that I am starting to turn into my mom and asking questions about how food is prepared or where it is from when I go to restaurants...

KEY TAKEAWAYS:

- Buy organic foods to avoid added pesticides and hormones.
- Avoid foods that have been genetically modified.
- Check the labels on your produce to ensure that you are buying organic.

CHAPTER 7

NO DAIRY

———

"What do you want for dinner?" my mother asked in the same dreaded tone as she knew I would probably turn down most of her suggestions.

"Something good."

This was my most classic answer to this question that inevitably drove my mother crazy.

My mom would give me "the look," and I knew I had to come up with something or else she'd make me a salad for dinner.

And after two hours of field hockey practice, salad was the last meal I wanted.

"Let's do grilled cheese and tomato soup," I responded, finally giving her a real answer to her question.

"That's my dairy girl, but how about some broccoli with that? You need some green on your plate," my mom would constantly say.

For as long as I can remember, my mom has made fun of me for being a "dairy girl."

I had to have TCBY's white chocolate mousse as a treat each week. There was a time period when the only foods I wanted to eat were Annie's mac and cheese and quesadillas. And, to top it all off, my favorite meal of all time is a grilled cheese with tomato soup, as mentioned above. If I'm being honest, it is my favorite because it's delicious and takes minimal effort to make.

So, if you would have asked me if I would cut dairy out my diet one year ago, I would have told you that there was no way in hell that I would be able to live without it.

Dairy was not only a staple in my diet; it was my diet.

The delicious taste of a spoonful of Ben & Jerry's Half Baked ice cream is not the only reason that avoiding dairy was so challenging for me.

In the last ten years, the United States has produced over forty-seven BILLION pounds of dairy each year.[58]

Dairy is everywhere.

Writer for The Spruce Eats Ashley Adams wrote an article that revealed many products contain hidden dairy in her article "Foods that Contain "Hidden" Dairy: If you are dairy-free, you may want to steer away from these products."

Among some of the products listed were cereal bars, a variety of breads, deli meats, and even some vegetarian meat replacements. Adams indicated that many of these products contain "casein, nonfat milk powder, or whey protein or whey protein isolates."[59]

Sometimes I was eating dairy, and I didn't even realize it.

"Well, have you tried minimizing dairy?"

Every time I would see a new dermatologist or esthetician, they would repeat this refrain.

I knew dairy was not the best for the skin.

---

58   Shabandeh, M. "Milk Retail Sales in the United States from 2005 to 2018 (in Billion Pounds)." Statista, June 26, 2019.

59   Adams, Ashley. "If You Are Dairy-Free, Beware of These 11 Foods With Hidden Dairy." The Spruce Eats. The Spruce Eats, February 7, 2019.

Unfortunately, my mom and I both knew giving up dairy would be a near-impossible task for me.

But I did try to give up all dairy my junior year of high school, before I made the decision to go on Accutane.

However, as a sixteen-year-old who loved going to the local diner for black and white milkshakes and getting nachos as an appetizer, cutting out dairy was not realistic.

As I got older, my palette expanded, but dairy still remained a staple in my diet.

When I moved to Dallas, I became friends with my first completely lactose intolerant friend, Megan. I would be lying if I didn't say eating out with her was a serious adjustment.

I don't know how many times I would say, "Let's go get ice cream," after one of our Wednesday night master's classes, and she would give me the same look and say, "I don't eat dairy."

I would immediately respond with an "I'm sorry," and suggest an alternative late-night treat.

It wasn't that I did not care about Megan's dietary restrictions; dairy was just such a huge part of my diet that I couldn't imagine never having ice cream or pizza!

However, as this foreigner to dairy started to become my best friend, I had to adjust.

It started small. We would get poke for dinner because that would be weird with cheese, anyway. Then, when we would get takeout, we would get a salad without cheese.

And, soon, the big steps came. We would get pizza topped with dairy-free cheese and buy vegan cheese for our crackers during wine night.

Thanks to Megan, I started to realize that cutting out dairy was not as hard—or unsatisfying—as I once thought.

I started to eliminate real cheese or ice cream, and I completely cut out butter and milk.

And, if I'm being honest, now I prefer the taste of coconut milk ice cream and creamer to cow's milk products.

Even though Megan opened my eyes to incredible dairy-free products and accommodating restaurants in Dallas, I was not completely convinced to stop buying mozzarella cheese for myself until I started all of my research.

Anthony William put dairy on his famous "Do Not Eat List."

When I started to change my diet, my mom said she knew it would be hard for me to give up, but it was probably what I should eliminate first.

I quickly realized most of the doctors and researchers I respect gave similar advice to that of the Medical Medium. To say I was not pleased would be an understatement.

Darryl D'Souza included milk on his "foods that ruin our health" list.[60]

Chris Wark made it clear you should not be adding cheese to your salads.[61]

Nicolette Richer advises not to eat any foods that are derived from an animal.[62]

The McDougall program explicitly states that the diet does not include red meat, poultry, dairy products, eggs, and fish

---

60 D'Souza, Darryl. "Common Foods that ruin our Health." Essay. In Become Healthy or Extinct!, 6th ed., 120-125, 2019.

61 Wark, Chris. "Heroic Doses." Essay. In Chris Beat Cancer, 1st ed., 138-139. Carlsbad, CA: HAY HOUSE, INC, 2018.

62 Richer, Nicolette. "Eating Real." Essay. In Eat Real to Heal: Using Food as Medicine to Reverse Chronic Diseases from Diabetes, Arthritis to Cancer and More, 60-61. Coral Gables, FL: Mango, 2018.

because they "provide toxic levels of fat, cholesterol, protein and, very often, infectious agents and harmful chemicals."[63]

And this was just the beginning. Hyman and McDougall both undermined the reason why we think dairy is good for us—because it is a great source of calcium.

McDougall explained on his website that "plant foods contain generous amounts of calcium. A cup of cooked collard greens contains about 360 mg of calcium, while a cup of milk contains about 300 mg. A cup of cooked kale contains 210 mg. There is NO disorder known as "dietary calcium deficiency" – in other words, there is plenty of calcium in all plant food diets to meet the needs of both children and adults alike."[64]

In part two of *Food: What the Heck Should I Eat?* Dr. Hyman stated that "vegetables are actually a much better source of calcium. And despite the 'conventional wisdom, also known as dairy industry propaganda, high intake of milk are linked to *higher* rates of osteoporosis."[65]

---

63 McDougall, John. "A Revelation: Your Health Is Not Determined by Heredity." Dr. McDougall's Health & Medical Center. John A. McDougall. Accessed October 9, 2019.

64 McDougall, John. "Plant Foods Provide the Nutritional Building Blocks for Optimum Health." Dr. McDougall's Health & Medical Center. John A. McDougall. Accessed October 10, 2019.

65 Hyman, Mark. "Milk and Dairy." Essay. In *Food: What the Heck Should I Eat?*, 76. New York, NY: Little Brown & Co, 2018.

Many people drink milk to build strong bones, not to make their bones WEAKER! This research was shocking to me.

Hyman explained that dairy is bad for you because it is difficult for MOST adults to digest and metabolize lactose

He wrote that "about 70 percent of the world's population can't digest dairy, and for many others it can cause cancer, autoimmune disease, and acne."[66]

SEVENTY PERCENT!

That statistic is alarming. But it's not even the worst part.

As Hyman said, dairy has been shown to cause cancer. This is because many dairy products contain IGF-1, which is an "insulin-like growth factor." Researchers have found that IGF-1 is linked to "chronic kidney disease, diabetes, and heart disease," and "people with reduced levels of IGF-1 live longer and have lower rates of cancer."[67]

---

66 Hyman, Mark. "Milk and Dairy." Essay. In *Food: What the Heck Should I Eat?*, 77. New York, NY: Little Brown & Co, 2018.

67 Hyman, Mark. "Milk and Dairy." Essay. In *Food: What the Heck Should I Eat?*, 84-85. New York, NY: Little Brown & Co, 2018.

Once I discovered you could get calcium from vegetables and that research has shown that IGF-1 in dairy products helps cancer cells grow, I knew cutting out dairy needed to be a priority.

However, if you think it is completely unrealistic or you love cheese too much, Hyman and Li did have a few suggestions for products to buy.

- "Unsweetened grass-fed sheep, goat, or cow yogurt:"
  - Li and Hyman agreed yogurt can be beneficial to our health.
  - Hyman did specifically say that you should buy "grass-fed sheep, goat, or cow yogurt" that is "unsweetened and with live cultures."[68]
  - Li also said, "Yogurt in its pure form (without added sweeteners) is considered healthy food."[69]
  - If you avidly eat yogurt for breakfast, you can sweeten the yogurt yourself with local honey or add a gluten-free granola.
- Cheddar cheese and Gouda cheese:
  - Li included a list of cheeses people have eaten during research studies and showed positive results. The two

---

68 Hyman, Mark. "Milk and Dairy." Essay. In *Food: What the Heck Should I Eat?*, 77. New York, NY: Little Brown & Co, 2018.

69 Li, William W. "Chapter 8 Feed Your Inner Ecosystem." Essay. In *Eat to Beat Disease: the New Science of How the Body Can Heal Itself*, 167. New York, NY: Grand Central Life & Style, 2019.

most common cheeses he named are Cheddar cheese and Gouda cheese.

- When I did a no sugar diet in high school, the only cheese that was allowed was aged Cheddar cheese.
- Li stated that Cheddar can "supply healthy gut bacteria for your microbiome."[70]
- He also wrote that Gouda has "probiotic properties."[71]

• Aged cheeses:
- Some of the diets that my mother followed also allowed her to have aged cheeses. This may be because when cheese ages, the lactose starts to break down.

• Grass-fed dairy products:
- In addition, Hyman expressed that, like meat, grass-fed dairy products are the way to go. He wrote that "it contains not only the best ratio of the essential fatty acids, but also the highest levels of carotene, vitamin A, and CLA, which has beneficial effects on metabolism."[72]
- When looking for grass-fed and humanely raised dairy products, Hyman gave a list of labels to look for. They include "Animal Welfare Approved, Certified

70 Li, William W. "Chapter 3 Microbiome." Essay. In *Eat to Beat Disease: the New Science of How the Body Can Heal Itself*, 45-47. New York, NY: Grand Central Life & Style, 2019.

71 Li, William W. "Chapter 8 Feed Your Inner Ecosystem." Essay. In *Eat to Beat Disease: the New Science of How the Body Can Heal Itself*, 166. New York, NY: Grand Central Life & Style, 2019.

72 Hyman, Mark. "Milk and Dairy." Essay. In *Food: What the Heck Should I Eat?*, 88. New York, NY: Little Brown & Co, 2018.

Humane, American Humane Certified, Food Alliance Certified, and Global Animal Partnership."[73]

Lastly, if you are going to make the choice to eat dairy and cannot stick to only eating unsweetened yogurt or cheddar cheese, there are a few products that Hyman advises you not to eat in his book.

According to Hyman, steer clear of processed cheeses and skim and low fat milk. The prepackaged cheeses like "Swiss, cheddar, and American...are full of hormones, allergens, and additives, and the fat in skim/low fat milk is replaced with 'sugar and artificial flavors.'"[74]

After looking for more dairy items to avoid, I also found on Medical News Today's website that I need to carefully read the labels on dairy products.

The website indicated that when reading the labels, look for "added sugars; added starch; thickeners, such as carrageenan; added flavoring; and preservatives."[75]

---

73 Hyman, Mark. "Milk and Dairy." Essay. In *Food: What the Heck Should I Eat?*, 91. New York, NY: Little Brown & Co, 2018.

74 Hyman, Mark. "Milk and Dairy." Essay. In *Food: What the Heck Should I Eat?*, 88. New York, NY: Little Brown & Co, 2018.

75 Johnson, Jon. "Dairy Alternatives: A Guide to the Best Dairy Substitutes." Medical News Today. MediLexicon International, October 22, 2018.

If you are wondering why a thickener like carrageenan is not recommended, Dr. Andrew Weil explains in his article "Is Carrageenan Safe?" that the ingredient has been linked to inflammation, ulcers, and inflammatory bowel disease.[76]

Megan has done an incredible job of living a satisfying dairy-free life.

She even started her own blog with her sister called "The Sister Squeeze," which includes many of her amazing dairy-free meals.

I am grateful I had Megan when I started my journey of cutting out dairy because I would have never known which restaurants offer dairy-free pizza or the best brands of vegan cheese.

Cutting out dairy is a process, but it could be necessary if you are a part of the seventy percent that cannot metabolize lactose, if you are fighting an illness, or if you don't want to develop ulcers in the future!

---

76 Weil, Andrew. "Is Carrageenan Safe?: Food Additives: Andrew Weil, M.D." DrWeil, July 8, 2019.

KEY TAKEAWAYS:

- Many doctors have not found that calcium from dairy is necessary and have discovered many reasons not to consume dairy.
- You can get enough calcium from eating vegetables.
- If you want to slowly eliminate dairy, stick to unsweetened, grass-fed products and aged cheeses.
- Check the labels! Make sure producers are not sneaking in harmful additives in your dairy or dairy in foods that are typically dairy-free.

CHAPTER 8

NO GLUTEN

———

"I want you to try the 'No Sugar Diet' for three weeks," my alternative health practitioner stated.

In my mind, I thought eliminating sugar would be relatively easy.

I just wouldn't be able to eat dessert.

Piece of cake.

However, I quickly learned that the "No Sugar Diet" cuts out any food that digests in your body as a sugar, which meant I could not have any bread.

I was a junior in high school when this diet was recommended to me.

As I mentioned in the "No Dairy" chapter, when I was about to start my treatment of Accutane, my mom wanted to ensure my body was strong enough to handle the potential side effects of the drug. She asked my alternative health practitioner to put me on a diet plan that would support me.

The only "bread" that was allowed was two slices of Ezekiel bread per day. And, let me tell you, I had my two slices every single day for the three weeks I followed the dreaded "No Sugar Diet."

I also had to limit my meat intake and couldn't have any starches, like potatoes.

At first, I did not like the taste of Ezekiel bread and could only eat it when it was toasted and had an egg or aged cheddar on top.

However, once the three weeks ended, my family continued to buy Ezekiel bread instead of whole wheat.

My family made this choice because of all of the benefits this type of bread contained.

According to Food For Life's website, Ezekiel bread is made out of wheat, barley, lentils, millet, soybeans, and spelt. The website also explains that the benefits of eating this bread include receiving a complete source of protein, eighteen amino acids, Vitamin C, Vitamin B, and fiber.[77]

The reason Ezekiel bread was allowed on the diet is because it does not contain flour, only certified organic grains.

Ezekiel bread continued to be my choice of bread in college and for some of the time that I lived in Dallas.

Now, I do not typically eat sandwiches or toast, so I do not purchase it as frequently. However, when I go to the beach and make sandwiches for lunch, Ezekiel gluten-free bread is still my go-to.

My choice to eat Ezekiel bread was one that was forced upon me, and then it became a habit. However, when I ate at restaurants or at other people's homes, I would eat any type of bread that I was given.

It was not until my family and friends needed to make dietary changes, and I started researching foods that impact our health, that I realized I should probably begin to cut out all gluten.

This was a daunting and unwelcomed realization.

---

77   "Ezekiel 4:9 Bread. and Better!" Food For Life. June 18, 2019.

I vividly remember reading the copy of *Liver Rescue* and flipping to the acne section.

As previously mentioned, acne has always been my biggest health battle. As I was reading the chapter on acne, I came across a section that explained that alternative medical practitioners blamed acne on eating too much dairy or wheat because both of these foods are "allergenic."[78]

However, Anthony William said it may be due to the fact that "strep loves wheat and dairy."[79]

After reading this line, I knew I was screwed.

I continued reading and came across another line that did not bring me much comfort.

Anthony William also wrote that the same strep that loves wheat and dairy and impacts acne also causes urinary tract infections.

It always seemed strange to me that every doctor I visited told me I am in great health, but they could not explain

78 William, Anthony. "Chapter 23 Acne." Essay. In Medical Medium Liver Rescue: Answers to Eczema, Psoriasis, Diabetes, Strep, Acne, Gout, Bloating, Gallstones, Adrenal Stress, Fatigue, Fatty Liver, Weight Issues, SIBO & Autoimmune Disease, 1st ed., 159. Carlsbad, CA: Hay House, Inc., 2018.

79 Ibid.

why I had horrible acne or why I got UTIs more than the average woman.

Wheat and dairy were cornerstones of my diet for as long as I could remember. It was no wonder I could not get rid of my acne or easily prevent UTIs.

I knew that if I wanted to heal my acne and persistent UTIs, I should take matters into my own hands and eliminate gluten and dairy.

The advice of Anthony William was confirmed by most of the books I read.

Darryl D'Souza has wheat on his "Foods that ruin our health" list.[80]

Nicolette Richer recommends you do not eat "food that has been sitting on a shelf for more than two days, like packaged crackers, cookies, breads and cereals" and "food that is refined, like flours, oils, beverages, etc."[81]

80 D'Souza, Darryl. "Common Foods that ruin our Health" Essay. In *Become Healthy or Extinct!*, 6th ed., 126-127, 2019.
81 Richer, Nicolette. "Eating Real." Essay. In Eat Real to Heal: Using Food as Medicine to Reverse Chronic Diseases from Diabetes, Arthritis to Cancer and More, 59. Coral Gables, FL: Mango, 2018.

Mark Hyman wrote in his book: "You don't *need* grains at all. You can get the nutrients they contain from other less problematic foods."[82]

So, what is the problem with wheat and grains?

Darryl D'Souza writes that our bodies were not meant to eat grains year-round, but only during the winter months when "fruits and vegetables do not grow."[83]

However, he reports that "having these foods in excessive quantities all year round, especially during the summer, damages the digestive tract and the mucosa in the long run."[84]

Hyman also writes that eating gluten damages our digestive tract.[85]

He writes that "many more of us are afflicted with NCGS - non-celiac gluten sensitivity - which is essentially an extreme inflammatory reaction to the same protein. Even those of us

82 Hyman, Mark. "Grains." Essay. In Food: What the Heck Should I Eat?, 187. New York, NY: Little Brown & Co, 2018.
83 D'Souza, Darryl. "The Right balance of Food." Essay. In *Become Healthy or Extinct!*, 6th ed., 55, 2019.
84 Ibid.
85 Hyman, Mark. "Grains." Essay. In Food: What the Heck Should I Eat?, 193. New York, NY: Little Brown & Co, 2018.

without celiac may damage the cells of our intestinal lining when we eat gluten."[86]

He even states that "recent evidence has found that anyone who consumes gluten may have a mild form of leaky gut."[87]

Even those of us who are not diagnosed with celiac disease or a gluten intolerance could be facing serious ramifications from eating bread or pasta.

We might overwork our pancreas when we eat so many grains.

D'Souza says that "if we eat grains all year - its round-the-clock conversion to sugar overworks the pancreas by forcing them to produce insulin every day, all year round. The insulin producing islet cells in the pancreas die from such fatigue and this causes Type I Diabetes."[88]

So...my favorite chocolate chip muffin could be damaging my intestines or making me at risk for diabetes?

That's honestly terrifying.

---

86 Ibid.
87 Ibid.
88 D'Souza, Darryl. "The Right balance of Food." Essay. In *Become Healthy or Extinct!*, 6th ed., 59, 2019.

We have been programmed from a young age to think oatmeal for breakfast, a sandwich for lunch, and a dish with brown rice for dinner is healthy and part of a well-balanced meal.

However, Hyman reports that "whole wheat bread usually contains very few whole grains," "oatmeal has a high glycemic index," "breakfast cereal should be called breakfast candy," and "nearly all the grains we consume today have been processed to death, so the good stuff they once contained is lost."[89]

I know that when I read this research I felt bamboozled.

Everything I grew up thinking was being challenged.

However, there are some better choices that you can make when it comes to eating grains if this research confuses you as much as it baffled me.

In Li's *Eat to Beat Disease*, he informs readers of the health benefits of some grains like "whole wheat barley, buckwheat, couscous, farro, oats, and quinoa."[90]

---

89 Hyman, Mark. "Grains." Essay. In Food: What the Heck Should I Eat?, 186-187. New York, NY: Little Brown & Co, 2018.

90 Li, William W. "Chapter 12 Rethinking the Kitchen." Essay. In *Eat to Beat Disease: the New Science of How the Body Can Heal Itself*, 284. New York, NY: Grand Central Life & Style, 2019.

Hyman also states that "black rice, quinoa, and buckwheat" are better choices if you are going to eat grains.[91]

GRAINS THAT ARE BETTER CHOICES:

- Whole Wheat Barley
- Buckwheat
- Couscous
- Farro
- Oats
- Quinoa
- Black Rice

In addition, Li suggests his readers eat pumpernickel bread because it "has a prebiotic effect that may decrease the population of toxin-generating bacteria in your gut, resulting in an overall healthier gut and body."[92]

If you are going to continue to incorporate grains in your life, Hyman urges readers to make sure they are "whole grains, organic, and gluten-free."[93]

91 Hyman, Mark. "Grains." Essay. In Food: What the Heck Should I Eat?, 187. New York, NY: Little Brown & Co, 2018.
92 Li, William W. "Chapter 8 Feed Your Inner Ecosystem." Essay. In Eat to Beat Disease: the New Science of How the Body Can Heal Itself, 174. New York, NY: Grand Central Life & Style, 2019.
93 Hyman, Mark. "Grains." Essay. In Food: What the Heck Should I Eat?, 201-202. New York, NY: Little Brown & Co, 2018.

Since I have cut out gluten, I only buy quinoa and try pastas that are made of chickpeas or red lentils. I also make sure that any "pasta" that I buy is organic and gluten-free.

One of my favorite brands is Tolerant Organic. Their "pastas" are delicious and only have one ingredient, so you know that you aren't eating any added preservatives or sugars. I also buy Siete Family Foods tortillas and use those to make wraps.

Luckily, there are so many gluten-free alternatives. Just make sure you are reading the ingredients, because a lot of gluten-free options add unnecessary sugar to the product.

KEY TAKEAWAYS:

- Ezekiel bread and pumpernickel bread are better choices if you want to keep bread in your life.
- There are grains, like quinoa, that don't have the same detrimental effects on your gut.
- Check the labels of gluten-free products for additives and sugars.

CHAPTER 9

NO MEAT

———

"You're an athlete—you need plenty of protein in your diet."

Sound familiar?

Ever since I was a young girl, it has been instilled in me that I need protein, especially when I was playing sports.

Every parent was always concerned with us girls getting enough protein.

Additionally, when you come from a family like mine that legitimately breeds athletes, it is hard to not follow this high-intensity workout and protein lifestyle. My parents cared so much about my athletics that I would go from soccer practice from 3:00 p.m. to 5:00 p.m. and then basketball practice from 6:00 p.m. to 7:30 p.m. twice a week—and that was just my schedule in the spring.

During this part of my life, I was eating so much protein. Honestly, a meal did not feel complete without some sort of meat. My salad had to have chicken on it, and we consistently ate turkey burgers and steak for dinner.

Anthony William explained that people believe they need to eat meat with meals to feel full because of the fat and not the protein.[94] I thought eating as much meat as possible was good for me and for building muscle.

One fact that did always stick out in my mind was that our serving size of meat should be the size of the palm of your hand.

Once I learned this fact, I realized eating so much meat might not be as healthy as I thought. From that point on, I did try to make a conscious effort to have small portions of meat— except when I downed a ten-piece Chicken McNuggets or enjoyed a juicy filet mignon.

It really was not until my best friend was diagnosed with a stage 4 thymoma that I learned more about meat's effect on the body.

---

94 William, Anthony. "Truth About Protein." Medical Medium Blog. Anthony William, Inc. , September 7, 2018.

Days after Trish was diagnosed with cancer, I started doing research on what foods someone battling her illness should eat. I remembered the times my mom cooked for both my grandparents when they were diagnosed with cancer and her preaching, "You need to feed your body good foods so that your body can fight."

I took on this same mind-set when Trish received the news about her cancer.

Thymomas are tumors caused by the autoimmune disease Myasthenia gravis. I did not—and still do not—know much about autoimmune diseases, but I did know people have used food to help manage them, like author Danielle Walker.

From the minimal research I did when Trish was diagnosed in March 2018, I learned that many meats contain saturated fats, which are not the best type of fat to consume, especially for people fighting for their lives.

Eating too many saturated fats is not recommended because they can contribute to a high cholesterol. Harvard Health Publishing wrote in the article "The truth about fats: the good, the bad, and the in-between" that saturated fats are found in red meat and dairy products and that "most nutrition experts recommend limiting saturated fat to under 10% of calories a day."[95]

Dr. Mark Hyman wrote in the "Meat" section of his book *Food: What in the Heck Should I Eat?* that the research on saturated fats leading to heart disease and high cholesterol has been disputed in some studies. He did say the jury is still out on the verdict on saturated fats and that we should continue to eat in moderation.[96]

However, most of the research I discovered on the Internet said that poultry and lean red meat are acceptable for cancer patients.

As I have mentioned, Trish is hands-down the pickiest eater I know, so I knew it would be no easy feat to get her to change her diet.

She recently wrote in an update that she used to refuse "to try any foods that weren't chicken fingers, pizza, ice cream, and Fruity Pebbles."[97] However, I wanted to make sure her body was strong when she underwent chemotherapy.

---

95   "The Truth about Fats: the Good, the Bad, and the in-Between." Harvard Health Publishing. Harvard Medical School, August 13, 2018.
96   Hyman, Mark. "Meat." Essay. In Food: What the Heck Should I Eat?, 33-42. New York, NY: Little Brown & Co, 2018.
97   Churchill, Trish. "Trish's Fight Against Thymoma." GoFundMe. GoFundMe, August 7, 2019.

When I created a Google Doc of food she could eat, the only meats on there were chicken and lean red meat.

Even though I had done some research and wanted Trish to stick to the foods on the Google Doc I created, I did not really follow these guidelines in my own home.

It wasn't until we received worse news that I realized I needed to step up my research and start to practice what I preached as well.

In July 2018, doctors told Trish her chemotherapy was not successful and that they recommended she stop treatment.

This news was devastating. She was basically told she had no options.

Surgery to remove the tumor was too risky and additional chemotherapy would be more harmful than beneficial.

We could not accept this news. We could not give up hope.

As a result, I decided to turn to the healthiest person we know: my mother.

My mother had just started following Anthony William and reading his book *Medical Medium Liver Rescue: Answers to Eczema, Psoriasis, Diabetes, Strep, Acne, Gout, Bloating, Gallstones, Adrenal Stress, Fatigue, Fatty Liver, Weight Issues, SIBO & Autoimmune Disease.*

The two words in that title that stuck out to me were "autoimmune disease." I thought this might be something that could help Trish, and immediately my mom Amazon Primed (is that a verb now?) us both a copy of the book.

Something that immediately stood out to me in Anthony William's book was that the recipes in the back did not include any animal products. There was not one recipe that included meat, fish, dairy, or eggs.

I knew I wanted to see what other researchers and doctors were saying about meat because I always thought protein was healthy.

In *Eat to Beat Disease: The New Science of How Your Body Can Heal Itself,* Dr. William Li wrote that "processed meat is considered a carcinogen by the World Health Organization."[98]

Chris Wark wrote in *Chris Beat Cancer* that "in 2015, the International Agency for Research on Cancer (IARC) classified

---

98   Li, William W. "Chapter 9 Direct Your Genetic Fate." Essay. In Eat to Beat Disease: the New Science of How the Body Can Heal Itself, 189-217. New York, NY: Grand Central Life & Style, 2019.

processed meats including bacon, sausage, ham, corned beef, canned meat, and jerky as Group 1 carcinogens."[99]

Yes, a carcinogen.

So why does a "healthy" or "well-balanced" meal consists of a sandwich in today's society if we know that processed meats are linked to cancer?

Many of the books I have read over the last few months have urged people to cut out most meat and stick to a more plant-based diet.

Chris Wark included a study in his book that looked at diets of middle-aged Americans. The study found that the participants who "reported eating a high protein diet were four times more likely to die of cancer or diabetes and twice as likely to die of any other cause in the next 18 years" than those on a plant-based diet.[100]

In *Eat Real to Heal: Using Food As Medicine to Reverse Chronic Diseases from Diabetes, Arthritis, Cancer and More* by Nicolette Richer, she recommends that her readers don't

99 Wark, Chris. "Heroic Doses." Essay. In Chris Beat Cancer, 1st ed., 126. Carlsbad, CA: HAY HOUSE, INC, 2018.
100 Wark, Chris. "Heroic Doses." Essay. In Chris Beat Cancer, 1st ed., 127. Carlsbad, CA: HAY HOUSE, INC, 2018.

eat any meat at all. She acknowledges that many people will be shocked by this recommendation because most people think eating meat is the way to get protein.[101]

Richer wrote that the "meat, dairy, and agricultural" industries have misled Americans about "the amount of protein your body needs to maintain health."[102]

In other words, eating meat is not the only way to get a sufficient amount of protein for our body to function because we don't need as much as we are told.

Richer goes on to add that too much protein actually shortens a person's life span. This danger may be due to the fact that animal protein is "high in calories, fat, pesticides, hormones, and antibiotics."[103]

I know these facts are not easy to read.

As I previously mentioned, I used to try to incorporate some type of animal protein into every meal.

101 Richer, Nicolette. "Eating Real." Essay. In *Eat Real to Heal: Using Food as Medicine to Reverse Chronic Diseases from Diabetes, Arthritis to Cancer and More*, 60-61. Coral Gables, FL: Mango, 2018.
102 Ibid.
103 Ibid.

It was not an easy adjustment to cut out most meats, so I gradually started to remove meat from my diet.

I began with what the Medical Medium put on his "Do Not Eat List." I stopped buying eggs, farm-raised fish, and pork.

These were the first three animal products I removed from my diet. It wasn't too difficult to cut these out. I never had time to eat breakfast before leaving for work at 7:00 a.m., and, aside from the occasional pulled pork sandwich, pork was not a huge part of my diet.

When I made the decision to cut out other meats, I knew I wanted to keep chicken, turkey, salmon, and yellowtail in my diet. These were the four most common animal products I kept in my apartment or ordered at a restaurant.

However, I did want to make sure I was only buying grass-fed and organic meat and wild caught fish.

In Hyman's *Food: What in the Heck Should I Eat?*, he explains why it is crucial for us to avoid factory farm animal products.

Factory farm animals are fed cheap grains, which means they could be eating genetically modified foods and pesticides. These animals are also "pumped full of hormones and antibiotics."[104]

To make matters worse, the additives that the Food and Drug Administration deem "safe" to eat would make your skin crawl.

The FDA defines an additive as any substance "the intended use of which results or may reasonably be expected to result, directly or indirectly, in their becoming a component of food or otherwise affecting the characteristics of food."[105]

As you can see, this definition is extremely broad and not very specific. The FDA's website also includes this note that "[because] of inherent limitations of science, FDA can never be *absolutely* certain of the absence of any risk from the use of any substance. Therefore, FDA must determine — based on the best science available — if there is a *reasonable certainty of no harm* to consumers when an additive is used as proposed."[106]

This statement is surely engineered to protect the FDA in court, but it is a concern for the rest of us that they do not know with total certainty the health impacts of what is directly or indirectly added to our food.

---

104 Hyman, Mark. "Meat." Essay. In Food: What the Heck Should I Eat?, 34. New York, NY: Little Brown & Co, 2018.

105 "Overview of Food Ingredients, Additives & Colors." U.S. Food and Drug Administration. FDA, April 2010.

106 Ibid.

When you eat factory farm meat, you are also eating everything the animal ate. If you are trying to actively avoid eating hormones, pesticides, and additives, then you need to actively avoid meat from factory farms.

I know a common criticism about eating grass-fed and organic meat is that it is expensive.

I get that.

I only have to feed myself on my teacher salary, and groceries can get pricey each month. Hyman addresses this issue in his book and makes the argument for spending a little extra on high quality food.

His best argument for spending an extra three to four dollars on quality, humanely raised meat is simple: "Reorganizing your budget to focus on your health and quality of food will make you feel better now and save much more in health care costs later."[107]

Making the decision to buy the best quality meat also helped me to stop relying on protein to keep me full. Because I needed to allocate more money on quality instead of quantity, eating meat became more of a treat and less of a necessity.

---

107 Hyman, Mark. "Meat." Essay. In Food: What the Heck Should I Eat?, 49. New York, NY: Little Brown & Co, 2018.

Once I started to feel satisfied from meals without meat, I became stricter with what I chose to buy.

In Li's *Eat to Beat Disease,* the only meat he recommends is chicken thighs. He wrote that as long as we trim the fat on the dark meat, it is a healthy option. Dark meat chicken thighs are high in vitamin K2. Li used two studies to show the benefits of consuming vitamin K2. One study showed how eating more K2 helped to inhibit prostate cancer growth and the other study showed that it reduced the risk of dying of heart disease.[108]

Because of the information in Li's book, I started only buying chicken thighs and salmon at the grocery store.

Li put simply in his book that "people who eat seafood live longer."[109] He listed many reasons why this fact may be true, including seafood contains omega-3 fatty acid, eicosatetraenoic acid, and docosahexaenoic acid.[110]

There were many other types of fish that Li explained had high levels of these fats, but salmon was honestly the only

108 Li, William W. "Chapter 6 Starve Your Disease, Feed Your Health." Essay. In Eat to Beat Disease: the New Science of How the Body Can Heal Itself, 112. New York, NY: Grand Central Life & Style, 2019.

109 Li, William W. "Chapter 6 Starve Your Disease, Feed Your Health." Essay. In Eat to Beat Disease: the New Science of How the Body Can Heal Itself, 109. New York, NY: Grand Central Life & Style, 2019.

110 Ibid.

fish I liked and knew how to cook. For more information on what seafood to eat, I highly recommend buying a copy of *Eat to Beat Disease.*

To sum it all up, even though the research is not concrete on whether we should cut out all meat or if we can continue to eat red meat, a few suggestions were uniform in almost every book or article I read.

In the last few months, Trish and I have made more of a commitment to stop buying meat at the grocery store.

Even though we knew all of the above research, what really pushed us to stop buying meat was the documentary on Netflix *What the Health.*

The documentary opened our eyes to some of the harsh realities of the meat and dairy industries.

My friend Maria was also impacted by this documentary. She told me "it was the information in that documentary that made me watch several other documentaries and read as much as I could about going vegan." Maria was immediately sold on several of the main themes of veganism like personal health, environmental impacts, and animal welfare. Through trial and error, she has made it her full-time lifestyle since March 2018.

When I moved to DC, I relied on Maria to tell me places she can eat out and hold me accountable for eliminating animal products while we are out. I feel so lucky to have Maria on my side as a health advocate.

The results she has seen from going completely vegan are impactful.

She explained to me that the most immediate change she experienced from changing her diet was having more energy.

In one conversation we had about being vegan, she said, "I truly felt alive and energized after a vegan lunch as opposed to hitting that 2:00 p.m. drag after eating a turkey panini and broccoli cheddar soup from Panera."

I think we all know that feeling after you have had a large, unhealthy meal and wish you could leave work and take a nap.

In addition to having more energy, she stated, "I think it also improved my quality of sleep because I woke up with a vitality that I never experienced before. After the first few weeks, my skin was the softest and clearest it has ever been. Being vegan has also gotten me to my healthiest weight with no fluctuation. I no longer have to worry about counting calories because as long as enough whole foods are included in the diet, I eat what I want, when I want, with no remorse."

KEY TAKEAWAYS:

- Eat grass-fed and organic meat and wild caught fish.
- Consume your protein in moderation. You do not need meat, fish, or an animal product during every meal.
- Do not eat processed meat!

I recommend you cut out the meats you do not love and go from there. Figure out what works for you—and your budget. It took Trish, Maria, and me time to cut out meat, so don't feel pressured to immediately eliminate all animal products.

CHAPTER 10

MAYBE EGGS, CORN, AND COOKING OIL

———

When you think of the all-American breakfast, what comes to mind?

I know I think of pancakes, eggs, bacon, and toast. And, if you're like me, you prefer your eggs scrambled with cheese.

I mean, the American breakfast sandwich is a bacon, egg, and cheese, or, depending on where you're from, a Taylor Ham, egg, and cheese.

This all-American breakfast includes the three foods I have been advising to cut out of your diet: gluten, dairy, and meat.

However, these foods are three staples in the American diet.

At your family's Fourth of July barbecue, while you are celebrating America, I am sure you have hamburgers, hot dogs, and corn on the cob.

Corn on the cob has become a summertime go-to side dish.

This chapter might have you question some of these other essentials in the "American" diet.

Anthony William included eggs, corn, and Canola oil on his "Do Not Eat List."

When I saw eggs and corn on there, I was stumped.

I ate an egg white omelet with broccoli, spinach, and cherry tomatoes for breakfast every weekend. I did not eat corn by itself typically, but I did have corn tortilla chips with guacamole or pupusas as a snack.

I needed to read more about why these foods were detrimental to your health and what doctors and researchers were recommending.

Let's start with eggs.

One reason that Chris Wark cut out eggs was because they contain methionine. Cancer cells depend on this amino acid, and animal foods, including eggs, have the "highest levels" of methionine.[111]

The McDougall program does not include any animal foods.

Nicolette Richer does not recommend eating eggs because your body doesn't need them, along with other animal products.[112]

Dr. Mark Hyman was the only one to mention some of the pros and cons of eggs and offer tips on how to pick the best-quality eggs.

Hyman warns readers about eggs because they are the number two cause of "reported outbreaks of food-borne illness."[113]

Warning: the reason is gross.

111 Wark, Chris. "Heroic Doses." Essay. In Chris Beat Cancer, 1st ed., 127. Carlsbad, CA: HAY HOUSE, INC, 2018.

112 Richer, Nicolette. "Eating Real." Essay. In *Eat Real to Heal: Using Food as Medicine to Reverse Chronic Diseases from Diabetes, Arthritis to Cancer and More*, 60-61. Coral Gables, FL: Mango, 2018.

113 Hyman, Mark. "Poultry and Eggs." Essay. In Food: What the Heck Should I Eat?, 69. New York, NY: Little Brown & Co, 2018.

"Eggs are typically contaminated either when the chickens that produce them carry harmful bacteria or when bacteria-laden feces come into contact with the egg-shells."[114]

If you choose to eat eggs, you need to be sure you are washing the shell before you crack them on your bowl or pan because "bacteria-laden feces."

No, thank you.

In addition to washing your eggs, you should also be sure that you buy one hundred percent "pasture-raised" eggs. You want eggs from "pastured hens that were fed an organic diet, and you want them as fresh as possible."[115]

Eating pasture-raised eggs will decrease your chances of coming in contact with chemicals, toxins, or bacteria.

I personally did not have a hard time eliminating eggs from my diet—or so I thought.

I stopped buying egg whites and putting hard-boiled eggs into my salads. However, the difficult part about eliminating

114 Hyman, Mark. "Poultry and Eggs." Essay. In Food: What the Heck Should I Eat?, 69-70. New York, NY: Little Brown & Co, 2018.

115 Hyman, Mark. "Poultry and Eggs." Essay. In Food: What the Heck Should I Eat?, 72. New York, NY: Little Brown & Co, 2018.

eggs from my diet was not being able to buy products made with eggs.

Many gluten and dairy-free desserts are made with eggs, and a lot of veggie burgers contain eggs, too. It was clear I would have to start buying vegan products to ensure eggs would not be an ingredient that was used.

Then, I started to run into another problem.

Corn.

Many of the products that did not have egg, gluten, or dairy contained cornstarch.

I vividly remember finding gluten–, dairy–, egg–, and soy-free onion rings, and I was so excited. I got them home and went to cook them.

I took the bag out of my freezer, checked the ingredients more carefully, and discovered the base of the onion ring's shell was made with corn—I probably should have done a better job of checking the label before purchasing those.

I was so upset because I felt like every time I found a product I could eat, one of the items from Anthony William's "Do Not Eat List" would show up.

I am still not totally sure what I think about corn.

Many of the books I read did not mention it. The only author who put corn on a list of foods to eat was Nicolette Richer.[116]

Chris Wark and Dr. William Li did not include corn on their lists of foods that beat cancer or disease.

Hyman noted that corn is ranked "high on the glycemic load list."[117] However, he did not include corn on his "What the Heck Should I Eat?" list or his "What the Heck Should I Avoid?" list.

I would say proceed with caution when buying products that are made with corn or eating corn in general.

I choose to avoid it because the Medical Medium's blog post titled "Healing Acne" stated that "corn, in any amount, can feed strep in your system. Avoid corn and corn products while healing your cystic acne."[118]

---

116 Richer, Nicolette. "Eating Real." Essay. In Eat Real to Heal: Using Food as Medicine to Reverse Chronic Diseases from Diabetes, Arthritis to Cancer and More, 58. Coral Gables, FL: Mango, 2018.
117 Hyman, Mark. "Vegetables." Essay. In Food: What the Heck Should I Eat?, 126. New York, NY: Little Brown & Co, 2018.
118 William, Anthony. "Healing Acne." Medical Medium Blog. Anthony William, Inc. , June 22, 2017.

One of my main goals is to heal my acne and acne scars, so I am not taking any chances.

Also, Darryl D'Souza does warn readers against using corn oil when cooking.[119]

Could this be because corn isn't the best for us?

Other cooking oils D'Souza says ruin your health are "Groundnut, Canola, Corn, Hemp Seed, Flax, Sunflower, Olive, Safflower, Sesame as well as Butter and Lard."[120]

Some of the cooking oils Hyman said to avoid were "soybean oil, corn oil, safflower oil, sunflower oil, palm oil, peanut oil, and vegetable oil."[121]

I have read some conflicting research regarding whether some of these oils are that terrible for you.

However, one fact every researcher agreed on is that vegetable oils and canola oil are detrimental to your health.

---

119 D'Souza, Darryl. "Free Radicals and Antioxidants." Essay. In *Become Healthy or Extinct!*, 6th ed., 93, 2019.

120 D'Souza, Darryl. "Common Foods that ruin our Health." Essay. In *Become Healthy or Extinct!*, 6th ed., 132, 2019.

121 Hyman, Mark. "Fats and Oils." Essay. In *Food: What the Heck Should I Eat?*, 169-170. New York, NY: Little Brown & Co, 2018.

Dr. John McDougall includes information about how the fats found in vegetable oils "have been shown to depress the immune system, increase bleeding and promote cancers, especially those of the colon, prostate and breast."[122]

Hyman reports that "refined vegetable oils promote inflammation and may increase the risk of heart disease, suicide, homicide, and violent behavior."[123]

Who knew vegetable oils could be tied to so many problems?

I definitely did not.

I mean look at the name—VEGETABLE oil. Sounds healthy to me.

As I said before, canola oil is also a popular oil experts are warning us to stay away from. One reason might be because canola oil is "refined and bleached with strong chemicals and high heat."[124]

---

122 McDougall, John. "Fat & Cholesterol: Primary Poisons." Dr. McDougall's Health Medical Center. John A. McDougall. Accessed October 10, 2019.

123 Hyman, Mark. "Fats and Oils." Essay. In Food: What the Heck Should I Eat?, 147. New York, NY: Little Brown & Co, 2018.

124 Flores, Vanessa. "Why You NEED to Eat Fat to Lose Weight." Strong4ByV. Strong4ByV, September 27, 2018.

Unfortunately, canola oil is EVERYWHERE. If you read the labels of popular brands of chips or snack foods, almost all of them are made with canola oil. When you eat out at restaurants, most places cook with canola oil.

I thought canola oil would be the easiest food on Medical Medium's "Do Not Eat List" to eliminate because I don't cook with it at home, but I was sadly mistaken.

Next time you are out at a restaurant, you should ask what type of oil they cook your food in. Unless you are at an organic, vegan, or very health conscious restaurant, I bet they will say that they use canola oil.

Fortunately, if you are cooking at home, there are plenty of other oils that you can use.

Hyman and Li both rave about extra virgin olive oil in their books.

Li explains that EVOO is preferable because it "is made from pressed olives without any chemicals or refinement and contains the highest levels of bioactives, as well as best taste."[125]

---

125 Li, William W. "Chapter 6 Starve Your Disease, Feed Your Health." Essay. In Eat to Beat Disease: the New Science of How the Body Can Heal Itself, 118. New York, NY: Grand Central Life & Style, 2019.

Hyman states that "olive oil is practically a miracle food, as everybody knows, full of healthy fats, polyphenols, antioxidants, and anti-inflammatory compounds."[126]

So, olive oil tastes good and is good for us. That's a win!

However, there are two warnings that Hyman gives about EVOO. The first is that it has a "low smoke point," so it is "best when used raw, in dressings, or in sauces and gravies slow-cooked over low heat."[127]

He also tells readers that "an estimated 70 percent of what is sold in America as extra virgin olive oil has been adulterated, either with lesser-quality oil or something else altogether, like nut or soybean oil."[128]

One way that you can try and rectify this risk is by following Li's advice on the type of extra virgin olive oil to buy. He recommends the brands "Koroneiki (Greece), Moraiolo (Italy), or Picual (Spain)."[129]

---

126 Hyman, Mark. "Fats and Oils." Essay. In Food: What the Heck Should I Eat?, 161. New York, NY: Little Brown & Co, 2018.

127 Ibid.

128 Ibid.

129 Li, William W. "Chapter 6 Starve Your Disease, Feed Your Health." Essay. In Eat to Beat Disease: the New Science of How the Body Can Heal Itself, 118. New York, NY: Grand Central Life & Style, 2019.

And, if you are wondering what to use instead of olive oil when you are cooking, the answer is coconut oil!

I use coconut oil if I am sautéing or roasting. Not only is coconut oil safer to cook at a higher temperature, according to Hyman, but it also has many benefits. Hyman says coconut oil raises "good cholesterol," improves "quality and size and type of cholesterol," boosts metabolism," and "improves cognitive function."[130]

I have taken Hyman's advice, and I use organic extra virgin olive oil in salad dressings and coconut oil when I am cooking.

According to Hyman, other common oils to use raw are "flax oil, hemp oil, and macadamia oil" and use organic avocado oil if you are cooking at a high temperature.[131]

If you are trying to cure an illness or heal, I recommend avoiding eggs, corn, and canola oil.

I have been able to find premade foods without these ingredients and have found ways to use substitutes in my own

---

130 Hyman, Mark. "Fats and Oils." Essay. In Food: What the Heck
       Should I Eat?, 162-163. New York, NY: Little Brown & Co, 2018.
131 Hyman, Mark. "Fats and Oils." Essay. In Food: What the Heck
       Should I Eat?, 169. New York, NY: Little Brown & Co, 2018.

home. For example, you can use applesauce or cashew butter instead of eggs in baked goods and arrowroot flour instead of cornstarch.

KEY TAKEAWAYS:

- Avoid eggs and corn if you can. There is research that shows they are harmful and not much that shows they are beneficial.
- DO NOT use vegetable oil or canola oil.
- Buy organic extra virgin olive oil and organic virgin coconut oil for your home.

PART 3

WHAT ELSE CAN I DO?

CHAPTER 11

YES CHEWING, JUICING, AND BLENDING

———

"Chewing your food is not that important. That's what your digestive system is for," stated my roommate Jason as we were day drinking at our apartment complex's pool.

Jason is an extremely intelligent guy. I mean, he chose to live with me for two years, so clearly he knows how to make informed decisions.

However, I had just finished researching information for this book, and I was ready to defend the importance of chewing your food to Jason.

I retaliated by stating "when you chew your food well or juice your produce, you give your body the maximum amount of nutrients that it can receive."

I know, this is a very nerdy conversation to have while you are drinking at the pool.

Many of the doctors and researchers discuss the importance of chewing your food well, blending your smoothies, or juicing your fruits and vegetables to get the greatest number of vitamins and nutrients.

This advice is something I originally never really thought about—but I could not admit that to Jason.

I used to completely agree with my roommate and figured your digestive system does its thing and your body absorbs the nutrients. And, while that may be true, there are ways to maximize the benefits of your food.

The first is by chewing your food well. But what does that even mean?

Darryl D'Souza discusses in depth why we need to chew our food and how it digests in his book *Become Healthy or Extinct.*

To summarize, he says you must chew our food well to ensure "that food gets mixed well with the enzymes in your saliva, and the size of the food particles also get reduced considerably, enabling digestive juices in later stages to work faster."[132]

The research Chris Wark shares in *Chris Beat Cancer* also supports what D'Souza writes. Wark wrote "the better you chew before you swallow the more nutrients you will absorb."[133]

As I said before, I do not really know what chewing "well" or "better" means; however, I do know that it is not scarfing down your food as fast as you can.

I also know we are always eating on the move.

When I was teaching at my last school, we would have thirty minutes for lunch, which was more like fifteen minutes once you factor in taking your class to lunch and picking them up.

That really does not give you that much time to sit there and chew your food until your cheeks hurt. However, I would say that, when you can, be mindful of how long you are taking to chew and enjoy your food. Your body will thank you later!

---

132 D'Souza, Darryl. "Digestion." Essay. In *Become Healthy or Extinct!*, 6th ed., 100, 2019.

133 Wark, Chris. "Heroic Doses." Essay. In Chris Beat Cancer, 1st ed., 130. Carlsbad, CA: HAY HOUSE, INC, 2018.

What is even better than chewing your food well is juicing.

Wark says that "juicing releases approximately 90% of the nutrients in food, about 3 times more than you can with your teeth."[134]

In *Eat Real to Heal,* Nicolette Richer explains that "one of the main reasons that people get sick is that they're eating plenty of food, but they're not absorbing the nutrients well."[135]

She explains that there can be quite a few explanations for this. However, one of them could be that "you lack the digestive enzymes and acids to break down your food into easy-to-absorb rations."[136]

I personally have struggled with digestion for almost my entire life; I just did not realize it.

When I talked to my alternative medicine practitioner about the symptoms I was feeling, like nausea in the morning—no, I was not pregnant—and exhaustion after getting a full

---

134 Wark, Chris. "Heroic Doses." Essay. In Chris Beat Cancer, 1st ed., 130. Carlsbad, CA: HAY HOUSE, INC, 2018.

135 Richer, Nicolette. "Nutrient Absorption." Essay. In *Eat Real to Heal: Using Food as Medicine to Reverse Chronic Diseases from Diabetes, Arthritis to Cancer and More,* 111. Coral Gables, FL: Mango, 2018.

136 Ibid.

night's rest, she said I probably was not getting enough nutrients from my food.

She suggested a few supplements to help me digest food and absorb the nutrients, but my goal is to have such a nutritional diet and well-functioning body that I do not need to rely on so many supplements.

All of this is to say I know the side effects of not getting enough nutrients from your food, and it is not pretty. It leads to a lot of cranky mornings and pulling up to work at 7:31 a.m. when your morning huddle started at 7:30 a.m.

Richer recommends that her readers juice and cook food "long and low" so that they can absorb the maximum nutrients.[137]

For all of you science people, she says that when we juice, "the nutrients travel through the body through osmosis, get absorbed into the system quickly, and are utilized by the mitochondria in the cells, tissues, bones, and all parts of the body."[138]

I wish I had that quote on hand when I was arguing with Jason. He is a science teacher after all.

---

137 Ibid.
138 Richer, Nicolette. "Nutrient Absorption." Essay. In *Eat Real to Heal: Using Food as Medicine to Reverse Chronic Diseases from Diabetes, Arthritis to Cancer and More*, 111. Coral Gables, FL: Mango, 2018.

If the science of digestion doesn't speak to you, you might be like me and prefer convenience.

I would much rather drink a juice or smoothie than eat a cup of spinach or munch on eight strawberries. It is so much easier to throw it all into my juicer or blender than pick at a bowl of fruit or figure out how I want to prepare my spinach.

So, when you make a smoothie or juice, you save time in your life and for your digestive tract.

That's what I call a win-win.

One juice that Alexandra, my mom, Trish, and I all drink is celery juice. We all drink sixteen ounces of pure celery juice every morning.

Anthony William recommends on his Medical Medium blog that you drink celery juice on an empty stomach. He also recommends that you wait at least fifteen minutes after drinking the celery juice before eating breakfast.[139]

We all started drinking celery juice because Anthony William states it is "beneficial for people who suffer from chronic and mystery illnesses." It has "powerful anti-inflammatory properties," is

---

139 William, Anthony. "Celery Juice." Medical Medium Blog. Anthony William, Inc. , May 24, 2018.

"able to starve pathogens," "supports the central nervous system," "strengthens the hydrochloric acid in your gut," and more.[140]

My best friend and roommate in DC, Carolina, recently started celery juicing with me every morning. She was inspired to start celery juicing to see if it would help heal her eczema.

The first time I juiced for her, she said she even enjoyed the taste of celery juice!

I promise it is not as bad as it might seem.

The Medical Medium describes all the profound benefits of celery juice in his blog, books, and Instagram. I definitely encourage you to explore the literature that he puts out if you are interested in drinking celery juice daily.

One tip when juicing: make sure you wash your fruits and vegetables well. You only need to soak them in water for a few minutes and then rinse them off to clean them. If you don't trust that water will clean them well enough, you can also add a little baking soda to the water that you soak your produce in!

In addition to drinking celery juice daily, Alexandra, my mom, and myself drink Medical Medium's heavy metal

---

140 Ibid.

detox smoothie every day. The smoothie is designed to eliminate common heavy metals from our system like lead or mercury.

On his blog, Anthony William states that heavy metals "poison our bodies, and can inflict damage on virtually every system and organ."[141]

For this reason, we all drink this smoothie for breakfast. My mom has even turned the smoothie into a ~trendy~ smoothie bowl on occasion.

For more information on the heavy metal detox recipe, I implore you to follow @medicalmedium on Instagram.

Lastly, D'Souza notes that blending your food is an excellent option. He recommends blending because you "use the entire edible portion of the food unit" and "do not separate the pulp out."[142]

Simply said, when you blend your fruits and vegetables, you are still consuming the nutrients from the entire piece of produce.

---

141 William, Anthony. "Heavy Metal Detox Smoothie." Medical Medium Blog. Anthony William, Inc. , August 17, 2016.

142 D'Souza, Darryl. "Blending." Essay. In *Become Healthy or Extinct!*, 6th ed., 79, 2019.

I keep a variety of organic frozen fruit, organic frozen spinach and kale, and organic bananas in the house at all times, making it so much easier to make a quick smoothie when I need a snack after work, or something sweet on the weekend.

I hope that this chapter convinces you, and Jason, to be a little more mindful when you chew your food or to consider adding celery juice to your morning routine!

KEY TAKEAWAYS:

- Stay present while you are eating and chew your food well.
- Juice or blend your fruits and vegetables to help your digestive system give your body maximum nutrients from the produce.

CHAPTER 12

YES FASTING

———

"Wait...you and Steven haven't eaten anything in 4 days?" I asked in awe.

"Yeah...it's really not that bad after the first day. By the fourth day I feel normal and like I could keep going," Trish casually replied.

Fasting is one of the trends I read about that took me a while to get on board with.

I was so accustomed to the research that said to eat a lot of small meals throughout the day to lose weight and curb your hunger. I did not think intermittent fasting or fasting for a few days could be healthy or promote a healthy body image.

I also thought the idea of teaching, even interacting with, 150 seventh graders without eating or drinking anything besides water for one day sounded terrible.

No, it sounded near impossible.

However, after reading doctors and researchers promote fasting, and watching Trish and her boyfriend absolutely crush their fasts, I felt like it was something that I could try.

Trish said she got inspired to do the fast when she read *Chris Beat Cancer*. During her monthly fasts, she drinks celery juice in the morning, water throughout the day, and decaffeinated tea in the evening.

She also learned more about the specifics of fasting from a close friend. He advised her to do four-day fasts for three months in a row. He informed her that on the fourth day of the fast, her body hits ketosis and goes into survival mode. The energy stored in her body feeds the essential organs first and starts to starve the cancer cells. In addition, the weaker cells die off.

After that, Trish said it is advised you do fasts as maintenance. She continued to do the monthly fasts because, after doing the first few, she received a routine scan of her tumor.

The doctors found that her tumor shrunk.

However, the doctors attributed the shrinkage to a delayed reaction from the chemotherapy.

Trish believes the fast kickstarted her chemotherapy again and that's why her scan showed a smaller tumor.

She thought the fast directly contributed to shrinking the tumor.

Chris Wark's description of his fast in *Chris Beat Cancer* was also the first one that I heard about after Trish's boyfriend read the entire book, and took notes on it—what an angel.

Chris Wark was diagnosed with stage 3 colon cancer in 2003 and had emergency surgery to remove the tumor. After his surgery, the doctors recommended that he receive nine to twelve months of chemotherapy.[143]

In the video "Stage 3 Colon Cancer Survival Story" uploaded onto YouTube by ChrisBeatCancer, Wark said chemotherapy "would destroy my immune system," and that he saw how "ineffective it was."[144]

He did not want to do it.

---

143 *Stage 3 Colon Cancer Survival Story. ChrisBeatCancer.* YouTube, 2011.
144 Ibid.

He realized he did not want to put his body through that.

Instead, in the video he said he decided to go one hundred percent raw vegan, drank vegetable juice, took herbal supplements, ran, went to the sauna, and meditated. In addition to all of these life changes, he also fasted.[145]

In Chapter 11 of *Chris Beat Cancer*, he discussed fasts he underwent during his healing journey. He did extended juice fasts and shorter water fasts.[146]

Wark easily explained the benefits of fasting in his book. To summarize what he wrote, fasting gives your body a break from its normal digestion and burning of glucose to burning body fat, which could be helpful if you are trying to lose weight, but it can also be helpful if you are trying to kill cancer cells.[147]

Wark explains that healthy "cells are...reinforcing their defenses to protect themselves." However, "cancer cells are mutated cells stuck in growth mode and now they have a difficult time adapting" to your body's starvation mode.[148]

---

145 Ibid.

146 Wark, Chris. "Take Out the Trash." Essay. In *Chris Beat Cancer*, 1st ed., 183-187. Carlsbad, CA: HAY HOUSE, INC, 2018.

147 Ibid.

148 Wark, Chris. "Take Out the Trash." Essay. In *Chris Beat Cancer*, 1st ed., 183. Carlsbad, CA: HAY HOUSE, INC, 2018.

If you have cancer cells in your body, fasting could make it difficult for them to keep growing, which is the goal of many cancer treatments.

In addition to the above benefits, Wark writes that "fasting recharges your immune system and reduces levels of IGF-insulin and glucose."[149] So, even if you are not battling cancer, you can still experience other health benefits.

If fasting for two to four days sounds like a daunting task, you could also choose to fast for much shorter amounts of time by skipping a few meals each week.

In Chapter 11 of *Eat to Beat Disease*, Li reported that "restricting your calories increases life span." He explains that restricting calorie intake has anti-aging benefits, induces weight loss, and activates your health defense systems.[150]

Instead of recommending that you fast for days, Li recommends that you "skip breakfast or lunch a few days each week," which might be a more realistic option for those of us who can't imagine going without food for an entire day, or

---

149 Wark, Chris. "Take Out the Trash." Essay. In Chris Beat Cancer, 1st ed., 184. Carlsbad, CA: HAY HOUSE, INC, 2018.

150 Li, William W. "Chapter 11 The 5 x 5 x 5 Framework: Eating to Beat Disease." Essay. In Eat to Beat Disease: the New Science of How the Body Can Heal Itself, 274. New York, NY: Grand Central Life & Style, 2019.

who live busy lives and are already accustomed to skipping your lunch to work.[151]

I know that when I was teaching, I would drink celery juice in the morning, bring a big smoothie and tea to work, and would be fine until my planning period at 2:30 p.m. During my off period, I would have an apple, banana, or veggie burger to tide me over until dinner.

Other days, I would only have my celery juice in the morning and wait until my 11:00 a.m. lunch break to eat. You need to decide what will work for you during your workday if you commit to restricting your daily calories.

My best friend, Lauren, has also begun fasting during the day. She explained that "Monday through Thursday, she eats breakfast, skips lunch, has a small snack after work, and then consumes a normal sized dinner."

She has done this for a few months and has seen immediate results.

Lauren "lost about 10 pounds," even though she "wasn't try-ing to lose weight." However, by skipping lunch four days per

---

151 Li, William W. "Chapter 11 The 5 x 5 x 5 Framework: Eating to Beat Disease." Essay. In Eat to Beat Disease: the New Science of How the Body Can Heal Itself, 275. New York, NY: Grand Central Life & Style, 2019.

week, she found she does not get as hungry overall and fills up quicker, so she ends up eating less in general.

In addition to losing weight, she has felt a difference in her energy levels. When I asked her how she felt now that she fasts, she said, "I feel good. Before, I used to crash after lunch and go into a food coma. I would become so sleepy and unproductive, but now I work through the day no problem—when I get a good night's sleep."

Lastly, Lauren explained that fasting helped her navigate all of the free food offered at her office. Many of us know that when breakfasts or lunches are catered at the office, they often include bagels and cream cheese, pastries, sandwiches, pizza, or pasta.

Once Lauren started fasting, she realized she did not need to indulge in all of this food at the office, and it also made her feel healthier and energized throughout the workday.

If you feel like you need a road map or a guide to plan your meals, in Chapter 14 of *Eat to Beat Disease*, Li includes a seven-day sample meal guide with the recipes. His calendar makes skipping meals look easy and painless.

Trish and Steven have continued to fast for four days each month.

Her tumor has not shown any growth since, and she is hoping that the fasting will contribute to additional shrinkage.

Not only do we believe that fasting has helped Trish, but Kris Gunnars reported "10 Evidence-Based Health Benefits of Intermittent Fasting" for HealthLine. A few of his reasons included:

- "Intermittent Fasting Changes The Function of Cells, Genes and Hormones"[152]

- "Intermittent Fasting Can Help You Lose Weight and Belly Fat"[153]

- "Intermittent Fasting May Help Prevent Cancer"[154]

- "Intermittent Fasting May Help Prevent Alzheimer's Disease"[155]

These are just a handful of results doctors and researchers have seen from fasting.

---

152 Gunnars, Kris. "10 Evidence-Based Health Benefits of Intermittent Fasting." Healthline, August 16, 2016.
153 Ibid.
154 Ibid.
155 Ibid.

Fasting is just another way you can use food, or a lack of food, to add another layer of defense and keep you living your best life.

KEY TAKEAWAYS:

- Fasting for four hours or for four days can help give your body a break from digestion and time to focus on your healthy cells.

CHAPTER 13

MAYBE ALCOHOL

———

"I love you to the liquor store and back."

Last year on Valentine's Day, my dad— yes, my dad—gave me a card that read that quote written in cursive on the front cover.

If that doesn't scream love, or that I might have a problem, I don't know what does.

Just kidding.

Kind of...

Of course, most people know alcohol is a drug and is not the best for your liver. However, if you are like me and are a social person, you also know alcohol is inevitable in social situations.

As a twenty-three-year-old living in Dallas and visiting DC, Philadelphia, and New York City often, I was constantly surrounded by happy hours, pregames, birthday parties, wine tours, and the occasional "I had a bad day at work, let's get wasted" kind of nights.

It is honestly really hard to navigate drinking when you are trying to eliminate toxins from your body and cleanse your liver.

I would be lying if I told you that, when I went out with my friends, I didn't take the shooter they bought me or didn't accept a mixed drink at a party. I definitely wanted to keep up with my friends and did not want to feel left out because I changed my diet.

However, I had to start making it a priority to make better and smarter choices when it came to consuming alcohol.

The first thought I had was if I was going to stick to a purely gluten-free diet, I needed to include alcohol.

When I lived with Alexandra in college, she was gluten-free, so we had a handle of Tito's vodka on hand at all times. She would bring a flask with her to parties because we all knew the five dollar handle of vodka the frats served was not gluten-free.

So I knew Tito's vodka would be a better choice, at least when gluten was concerned. Unfortunately, I later discovered that if you are trying to cut out corn, Tito's is a corn-based vodka.

Other vodkas that are gluten-free are Smirnoff, New Amsterdam, and Ciroc. Along with vodka, I am also a fan of tequila.

I mean, who doesn't love agave?

Agave is healthy, right?

Upon research, I discovered the popular tequila brands that are gluten-free are Jose Cuervo, Patron Tequila, and Herradura Tequila. Herradura Tequila may not be a household name, but when I worked at a bar in college, they did promotions at our bar, so I feel some loyalty to the brand.

Also, if you are a basic bitch like me, you will be happy to learn that White Claw Hard Seltzer and Truly are gluten-free as well.

As you may know, many beers contain gluten, but a lot of hard ciders do not! My favorite hard cider brands are Angry Orchard and Woodchuck.

I am in no way saying any of these alcohol brands are good for you; however, if you are trying to make yourself feel better by sticking to a gluten-free diet, there are options.

In addition, wine is almost always gluten-free! And there has been significant research done exploring whether or not wine is healthy. I definitely wanted it to be healthy and turned to the experts for guidance.

One thing I love about Nicolette Richer's book, *Eat Real to Heal*, is that she answers so many common questions. She has an entire section titled "And What about Alcohol?", which is a question I know you have been asking.

She is transparent in this section about the studies regarding alcohol consumption. She states that some studies say drinking a moderate amount of alcohol or wine can be beneficial, and some are inconclusive. Her advice is to "pay attention to how things impact you."[156]

I think that this is sound advice. I know some of my friends are allergic to some types of alcohol, and I know some

---

156 Richer, Nicolette. "And What about Alcohol?." Essay. In *Eat Real to Heal: Using Food as Medicine to Reverse Chronic Diseases from Diabetes, Arthritis to Cancer and More*, 95. Coral Gables, FL: Mango, 2018.

alcohol gives me a raging hangover and others makes me feel completely fine.

I also need to pay attention to how alcohol affects me when I am detoxing, and I go out and drink. Typically, the next day I feel extremely anxious. My Sunday Scaries are on another level.

Alexandra told me that since she has gone completely vegan and plant-based, she feels anxious for days after drinking.

She is in a place now that she does not drink at all, even if she does feel left out, because she would rather feel healthy than nervous or ill.

The other piece of advice that Richer offers is to drink in moderation—but what does that really mean?—and take "a break every now and then."[157]

She simply states you need to "give your hardworking liver a break, rather than giving your liver more work to do."[158]

Personally, I believe this advice is good for everyone, whether you are fighting an illness, doing a cleanse, or not doing much

157 Richer, Nicolette. "And What about Alcohol?." Essay. In *Eat Real to Heal: Using Food as Medicine to Reverse Chronic Diseases from Diabetes, Arthritis to Cancer and More*, 96. Coral Gables, FL: Mango, 2018.

158 Ibid.

to improve your health. Just like you wouldn't want to sit in the sun every day and burn your skin, you don't want to exhaust your liver too often, either.

In Hyman's chapter about beverages, he discusses "The Bottom Line on Wine." He informs readers that "there's no shortage of large studies showing that people who consume small doses of alcohol, especially wine, are slightly less prone to disease."[159]

Calm down y'all, he said SMALL doses.

He also writes that people who drink alcohol in small doses "have longer life expectancies than teetotalers (maybe it's because they have more fun)."[160]

Hyman, I felt that one on a spiritual level.

Also, if you don't know what a teetotaler is, like I did not, it is a person who does not drink alcohol.

However, and I hate to write this, he does mention that "as the number of drinks you consume surpasses one or two daily, so, too, does your risk of mortality."[161]

---

159 Hyman, Mark. "Beverages." Essay. In Food: What the Heck Should I Eat?, 246. New York, NY: Little Brown & Co, 2018.
160 Ibid.
161 Ibid.

So, maybe one to two drinks is that moderation that Richer was talking about.

If drinking a small amount of alcohol makes you less prone to disease and helps you live longer, what is the best alcohol for you to consume?

Hyman seems to think red wine. It "contains antioxidants and flavonoids such as resveratrol and quercetin, which improve arterial health, reduce inflammation, and protect mitochondria."[162]

Great news ladies, your wine nights may be saving your life, not just your man's life who you are inevitably venting about.

Li also discusses the benefits of red wine, and specifically resveratrol, in *Eat to Beat Disease*.

Li promotes drinking in moderation like Richer and Hyman. He states the benefits of red wine do not come from the alcohol but "from the bioactives in the drink."[163]

162 Hyman, Mark. "Beverages." Essay. In Food: What the Heck Should I Eat?, 247. New York, NY: Little Brown & Co, 2018.

163 Li, William W. "Chapter 6 Starve Your Disease, Feed Your Health." Essay. In Eat to Beat Disease: the New Science of How the Body Can Heal Itself, 116. New York, NY: Grand Central Life & Style, 2019.

Li also states that red wine might also improve "the gut microbiome" and reduce "inflammation of the body."[164]

Li recommends three types of red wine, "Cabernet Sauvignon, Cabernet Franc, and Petit Verdot," because they have antiangiogenic effects on the body. This means the effect that food and drink have on your body starves your cancer cells or prevents tumors.[165]

RECOMMENDATIONS:

- If you are going to drink, choosing a glass of Cabernet might be your best bet! My mom recommends Frey's Organic Cabernet Sauvignon.

- Hyman notes in his book that beer, hard cider, and sugary cocktails should remain off-limits.[166]

- If you are making a mixed drink or cocktail, I recommend using fresh squeezed juice or organic juice with no added sugars.

---

164 Li, William W. "Chapter 8 Feed Your Inner Ecosystem." Essay. In Eat to Beat Disease: the New Science of How the Body Can Heal Itself, 182. New York, NY: Grand Central Life & Style, 2019.

165 Li, William W. "Chapter 6 Starve Your Disease, Feed Your Health." Essay. In Eat to Beat Disease: the New Science of How the Body Can Heal Itself, 115. New York, NY: Grand Central Life & Style, 2019.

166 Hyman, Mark. "Beverages." Essay. In Food: What the Heck Should I Eat?, 252. New York, NY: Little Brown & Co, 2018.

- My mom and Alexandra used to drink their own margaritas made out of tequila, filtered water, raw honey, and fresh-squeezed, organic lime juice. This recipe is a better option than using a premade margarita mix.

- Other options are to bring a flask of a gluten-free liquor to a party, bring a bottle of organic red wine to your wine night, or to just refrain from drinking.

If you aren't boring, you should still be able to have fun with your friends sober!

KEY TAKEAWAYS:
- Choose gluten-free alcohol.
- Limit the number of drinks you have in a day to one or two.

CHAPTER 14

IS CHANGING YOUR DIET ENOUGH?

———

Okay, so you've eliminated foods with pesticides.

You've stopped drinking milkshakes, and you're done with the standard "American" breakfast of eggs, bacon, and pancakes.

Now what? Is that enough?

Obviously, doing any of the above is a great start. Changing your dietary habits, and honestly lifestyle routines, are processes that take time.

However, if you are committed to eliminating as many toxins and carcinogens from your life as possible, there are a few more nuggets of wisdom I have taken from my research.

The first and most important piece of advice I read in *Eat Real to Heal, Eat to Beat Disease,* and *Become Healthy or Extinct* is get rid of all of your plastic containers and replace them with glass.

Li explained that "plastic will break down over time and contaminate food."[167]

And, honestly, if you keep up with the news, you know plastic straws are getting banned to save the turtles, so why wouldn't you ban all plastic to save yourself from contaminants?

Richer writes that you should even get a stainless steel juicer over a plastic one,[168] and Li says you should eliminate plastic utensils, tools, and cups.[169]

---

167 Li, William W. "Chapter 12 Rethinking the Kitchen." Essay. In Eat to Beat Disease: the New Science of How the Body Can Heal Itself, 281. New York, NY: Grand Central Life & Style, 2019.

168 Richer, Nicolette. "All about Juicing." Essay. In Eat Real to Heal: Using Food as Medicine to Reverse Chronic Diseases from Diabetes, Arthritis to Cancer and More, 96. Coral Gables, FL: Mango, 2018.

169 Li, William W. "Chapter 12 Rethinking the Kitchen." Essay. In Eat to Beat Disease: the New Science of How the Body Can Heal Itself, 281. New York, NY: Grand Central Life & Style, 2019.

Plastic may be extremely convenient to us, but at what cost?

An article by National Geographic "We Know Plastic Is Harming Marine Life. What About Us?" explores the idea that the plastic intake that marine life experience could also harm us.

The researchers have found that "microplastics damage aquatic creatures, as well as turtles and birds" because "they block digestive tracts, diminish the urge to eat, and alter feeding behavior, all of which reduce growth and reproductive output."[170]

Plastic also has chemical impacts on health because chemicals "tend to adhere to the surface" of plastic items.[171]

The article included a study done by professor Chelsea Rochman, who fed small fish contaminated plastic. She found that the fish who ate this plastic suffered from liver damage.[172]

And, as you know, the liver is key to our health.

If this is what microplastics are doing to sea creatures, could they be doing similar damage to us?

---

170 Royte, Elizabeth. "We Know Plastic Is Harming Marine Life. What About Us?" National Geographic, May 16, 2018.

171 Royte, Elizabeth. "We Know Plastic Is Harming Marine Life. What About Us?" National Geographic, May 16, 2018.

172 Ibid.

Does eating animals that have ingested microplastics and contaminants impact our health?

Could using plastic containers or utensils harm our liver health?

These are the questions I found myself asking after reading this report.

When I first read all of this, I was surprised. I knew you should not use plastic containers in the microwave, but I did not know they could be harmful for storing your food.

I also am the queen of convenience—well, laziness, but convenience sounds better.

I enjoy convenience so much that I kept a Costco-sized box of plastic utensils at my desk at work so that I never had to wash my silverware when I returned home.

However, after reading three separate authors report on the harm that using plastics can cause, I made the plunge and replaced all of my plastic containers with glass. I will admit I did wait until I used all of my plastic utensils at school and then started to bring my metal utensils from home. But, like I said, lifestyle changes take time, right?

If you can begin to eliminate the plastic cookware from your home, you will be better off.

In addition, Richer implores people who read her book to purchase stainless-steel pots and pans with water– or air-tight lids.[173]

Li advises readers buy "high-quality pans" which include ceramic coated, stainless steel, or cast-iron skillet or sauté pans.[174]

Along with eliminating plastic from your life, you can also eliminate the chemicals in your water—or at least try to.

Darryl D'Souza and Nicolette Richer discussed the pollutants that can come from our city's water pipes.

However, that might be just the beginning of our issues.

To clean our drinking water, the government uses chemicals. Even though some bacteria are eliminated from our water,

---

173 Richer, Nicolette. "Cooking Techniques." Essay. In Eat Real to Heal: Using Food as Medicine to Reverse Chronic Diseases from Diabetes, Arthritis to Cancer and More, 73-74. Coral Gables, FL: Mango, 2018.

174 Li, William W. "Chapter 12 Rethinking the Kitchen." Essay. In Eat to Beat Disease: the New Science of How the Body Can Heal Itself, 279. New York, NY: Grand Central Life & Style, 2019.

now, we have chemicals in our water, and we cannot be sure of the effect they will have on our bodies.[175]

Richer offers excellent advice in Part Three of *Eat Real to Heal*. She explains that there are different actions you can take to be sure you are not drinking unwanted chemicals and pollutants.

The easiest, and potentially cheapest, option is to purchase a Brita filter[176] . I personally have used a Brita for as long as I can remember.

If you would like to kick it up a few notches, she recommends that you purchase a drinking water test on Amazon.[177]

I decided to test the drinking water at my parents' house in Delaware. We found that the water from the sink was free of most of the metals and chemicals, except it had high rates of chromium and sulfate. Upon researching, I found

---

175 Richer, Nicolette. "Your Whole Health Plan." Essay. In Eat Real to Heal: Using Food as Medicine to Reverse Chronic Diseases from Diabetes, Arthritis to Cancer and More, 154. Coral Gables, FL: Mango, 2018.

176 Richer, Nicolette. "Your Whole Health Plan." Essay. In Eat Real to Heal: Using Food as Medicine to Reverse Chronic Diseases from Diabetes, Arthritis to Cancer and More, 155-156. Coral Gables, FL: Mango, 2018.

177 Richer, Nicolette. "Your Whole Health Plan." Essay. In Eat Real to Heal: Using Food as Medicine to Reverse Chronic Diseases from Diabetes, Arthritis to Cancer and More, 154. Coral Gables, FL: Mango, 2018.

that neither of these items are what you want to have in your water.

An article by Life Science titled "Chromium-6 in Tap Water: Why the 'Erin Brockovich' Chemical Is Dangerous" stated that "a national report released Tuesday (Sept. 20) found unsafe levels of chromium-6 or hexavalent chromium — known to cause cancer in animals and humans — in tap water across the country."[178]

We definitely did not want to take any risks, even if the chromium in our water was chromium-3, which is apparently safe.

When I was talking to Alexandra about her health journey over a vegan dinner in Philadelphia, we started talking about all of the lifestyle changes it takes to be healthy, or at least chemical-free.

She said she was listening to an interview with Anthony William, and someone asked him "What is the key to living a healthy life?" Alexandra told me he responded, "Clean air and clean water."

After hearing this interview, Alexandra knew she needed to make sure her water was clean.

---

178 Deamer, Kacey. "Chromium-6 in Tap Water: Why the 'Erin Brockovich' Chemical Is Dangerous." LiveScience. Purch, September 22, 2016.

I asked Alexandra what type of water filter that she uses, and she said she invested in a Berkey water filter.

I knew that this sounded familiar, and that was because that is the water filter that Richer suggested in *Eat Real to Heal*. Richer explained that the filter "catches 99 percent of contaminants while preserving the good minerals that you want."[179]

The Berkey water filters are on Amazon, and, I will admit, they are much more expensive than a Brita. However, if you take a water test and discover there are a lot of chemicals in water, you may want to make the investment.

My parents decided to buy a Berkey water filter after I tested the water at their house. They said that they would rather be sure that they were drinking clean water than wondering if the high levels of chromium and sulfate were harming them.

I tested the water after it had been filtered by the Berkey water filter, and the levels of chromium and sulfate in the water greatly decreased.

We knew we made the right decision by investing in the filter.

---

179 Richer, Nicolette. "Your Whole Health Plan." Essay. In Eat Real to Heal: Using Food as Medicine to Reverse Chronic Diseases from Diabetes, Arthritis to Cancer and More, 155-156. Coral Gables, FL: Mango, 2018.

One final recommendation that Richer made was to get an attachable filter to put on your shower.[180] The shower head attachments are extremely affordable on Amazon.

Richer explains that adding a shower filter is smart because "your skin is the largest organ of your body," and you want to make sure that the water that touches it everyday is "pure and uncontaminated."[181]

Again, if you are skeptical about making this purchase, I would test your water and see what you are putting on your skin every day!

As Anthony William said, clean water is not the only thing that is important—so is clean air!

My alternative medicine practitioner advised me to get an ionic air purifier and ozone generator when I was complaining about waking up feeling ill in my apartment in Dallas.

I purchased a small plug-in purifier on Amazon. I ran it twice a day, once in my bedroom and once in my bathroom. It was not very expensive, and it really did start to make a

180 Richer, Nicolette. "Your Whole Health Plan." Essay. In Eat Real to Heal: Using Food as Medicine to Reverse Chronic Diseases from Diabetes, Arthritis to Cancer and More, 156. Coral Gables, FL: Mango, 2018.

181 Ibid.

big difference on how I felt when I woke up in the morning. Instead of congested, fatigued, and nauseous, I started to wake up feeling well-rested and energized.

Shocking, I know.

I honestly listen to what my alternative medicine practitioner says without question, so I did not research the ionic air purifier before I bought one. However, after researching for this book, I discovered how the purifier works and some of the benefits.

On Air Oasis's website, they explain that an ionic air purifier uses "ions to remove particulates, microbes, and odors from the air."[182]

The site describes the process in detail by stating that "[air] ionizers create negative ions using electricity and then discharge them into the air. These negative ions attach to positively charged particles in the room, such as dust, bacteria, pollen, smoke, and other allergens. The positively charged particles and negative ions bond together to create dense dirt particles that cannot float in the air. These heavier dirt particles fall to the ground and wait to be swept up at a later time."[183]

---

182 "What Is an Air Ionizer?: Air Ionizer Benefits." Air Oasis. Accessed October 10, 2019.
183 Ibid.

By using ions to eliminate the contaminants in the air, you no longer breath them in.

Air Oasis says "air ionizers purify the air of bacteria, dust, cigarette smoke, molds, soot, pollen, and household odors."[184]

One word that stood out to me in the description was "molds."

Unfortunately, mold is way more common than we think, especially in apartments or older buildings. Trish and Alexandra both believe mold contributed to their illnesses because their homes were infected with a lot of mold.

Trish was even diagnosed with mold toxicity and was pre-scribed antibiotics to remove the mold from her lungs. Both of my friends had to move out once the inspectors discov-ered the mold.

Of course, I do not recommend that everyone go out and get their apartment or home tested for mold, but, if you want to take a precautionary step in case there is mold and other pollutants in your house, I recommend purchasing an ionic air purifier.

One more way to eliminate the chemicals in your life is to literally eliminate the chemicals from your home.

---

184 Ibid.

My parents own a janitorial supply company, Progressive Systems Inc. In 2011, they started to sell Earth Friendly Products, which is now called ECOS.

ECOS products are better for you because they have the Safer Choice label. According to the ECOS website, the "Safer Choice label help consumers and commercial buyers identify and select products with safer chemical ingredients, without sacrificing quality or performance. Earth Friendly Products is proud to have the highest amount of certified Safer Choice products in the US and to be designated as the EPA's Safer Choice 2017 & 2015 Partner of the Year."[185]

I personally love to use their Orange Plus All Purpose Cleaner and their Tea Tree Shower Cleaner.

In addition to using ECOS products, I also use Seventh Generation laundry detergent, toilet cleaner, and dish soap.

I like Seventh Generation because they use "plant-based ingredients, scents made from real ingredients, recycled packaging, and do not use synthetic fragrances or dyes."[186]

---

185 "Safer Choice." ECOS. Accessed October 10, 2019.
186 "Our Mission." Seventh Generation. Accessed October 10, 2019.

I actually switched to using Seventh Generation laundry detergent after I started to get rashes under my arms.

My alternative medicine practitioner told me that the detergent that I was using was causing a rash because it had too many chemicals in it. The rash went away completely within a week of switching to a pure detergent.

In addition, Richer recommends you stop using bleach and dryer sheets in your laundry room.[187] Both of these add extra chemicals and dyes that you do not need to ensure that your clothes are clean.

My mom even started to make her own cleaning products using Thieves cleaning products and Young Living essential oils. She makes dish soap, hand soap, and an all-purpose cleaner.

Thieves is another brand that ditches the chemicals and uses plant-based ingredients.

Making the switch to any of these cleaning products could help eliminate the chemicals in your home.

---

187 Richer, Nicolette. "Detoxifying the Home." Essay. In Eat Real to Heal: Using Food as Medicine to Reverse Chronic Diseases from Diabetes, Arthritis to Cancer and More, 144. Coral Gables, FL: Mango, 2018.

You can also eliminate chemicals you ingest by getting rid of scented candles and switching to essential oil diffusers. Pure Living Space's website indicates most scented candles are made with "paraffin, a chemically-bleached petroleum by-product." The website explains that "when you burn paraffin, it pollutes your air."[188]

Pure Living Space says if you want to keep candles in your home, make sure they are paraffin-free. They state that beeswax or soy candles are much less toxic for your home.[189]

Personally, I prefer using my essential oil diffuser and Young Living essential oils because I can change the scent daily.

On top of that, you can begin using chemical free hand soap, like Dr. Bronner's.

There are additional recommendations of natural products that I use in the "Recommendations" section of this book.

You do not need to change all of your household products or hygiene items right away. As you gradually run out of something, maybe try a product with a Safer Choice label.

---

188 "Thieves Products." Thieves Essential Oil Product Line | Thieves Oil Uses | Young Living Essential Oils. Accessed October 10, 2019.
189 Trimmer, Carol. "The Problem with Scented Candles & Your Health." Pure Living Space, December 8, 2017.

KEY TAKEAWAYS:

- Ditch the plastic kitchenware.
- Check your water and make sure your water filter is doing its job.
- Buy an ionic air purifier to make sure you aren't ingesting toxins.
- Switch to cleaning products and household items that contain less chemicals and dyes.

CHAPTER 15

MY MOM'S SUCCESS STORY

———

Could you imagine searching for a cure for your mystery illnesses for thirty years?

That is how long it took my mom, Gail, to find a diet and lifestyle that made her feel healthy.

In my Introduction I discussed Alexandra's ten-year healing journey.

Now, it is time for you to hear my mom's story.

My mom grew up in a typical Italian household with a lot of pasta and bread. Their home had everything from homemade pasta to rolls to fried bread. There was always a fragrant sauce made with pork, beef, or veal bubbling on the stove.

She also grew up in a lower– to middle-income household, consistently shopping with coupons.

My mom explained her family ate a lot of sugar cereals, TV dinners, and fruits and vegetables, too.

She informed me that her favorite snack foods were carrots and Tastycakes. Her breakfast consisted of Carnation breakfast drinks with milk or sugar cereal. For lunch, she would have peanut butter and jelly on white bread, chips, and Tastycakes. And, for dinner, there was usually a protein, a vegetable, and a starch. Except for Fridays, they would have whatever TV dinner was on sale at the store. And, every night, there was a dessert.

She has a brother and three sisters, and they were all obsessed with dessert. They still laugh about the fact that it was important to figure out what was dessert before deciding on what would be served for dinner.

As she got older and was in college and working, she ate whatever she wanted. She said she went out to eat a lot and lived on snacks.

My mother never experienced any side effects from this relaxed diet, except for bloating. She explained that no matter how skinny she was, she always had a little belly.

It wasn't until her late twenties that she started to feel differently.

She went to see an allergy doctor, in Lewes Beach, Delaware, and he diagnosed her with candida. According to Dr.Axe.com, "*Candida albicans* is the most common type of yeast infection found in the mouth, intestinal tract and vagina (vaginal/genital candidiasis), and it may affect skin and other mucous membranes."[190]

A yeast infection may not seem that serious.

However, Dr. Axe explains that "if the immune system is not functioning properly, the candida infection can migrate to other areas of the body, including the blood and membranes around the heart or brain, causing serious candida symptoms. This is referred to as invasive candidiasis."[191]

My mom was diagnosed with candida because she was experiencing bloating, fatigue, brain fog, and headaches. All of these are common symptoms of candida.

---

190 Axe, Josh. "Stop the Sugar Cravings and the Fuzzy Thinking!" Dr. Axe, January 25, 2019.
191 Ibid.

As you can imagine, owning and operating a start-up small business was challenging for my mom.

At this point, her many years of trying different diets and methods of healing began.

Her doctor put her on a candida elimination diet, which eliminated alcohol, caffeine, yeast, dairy, and mushrooms. She said she could eat meats and vegetables.

So, she started shopping in health food stores, drinking soy milk, and eating A LOT of eggs. In addition to the diet change, they put her on the drug Nystatin. According to Gail, this diet helps you get back to your "normal" weight. Her normal weight was 102 pounds—I wish I got those genes!

Although she started to feel better, she also began to feel alienated, questioned, and stressed about her food choices and food in general.

Friends and family did not understand her dietary restrictions, and there was a lot of eye rolling.

Welcome to my mother's high-maintenance life.

My mom explained she certainly did not choose to be "high-maintenance." She was taught by her parents to eat whatever was on her plate, and there were very few things that she didn't like to eat before starting to feel ill.

She stayed on this diet for three years, and then she got pregnant with me, at age thirty-two. My mom's pregnancy cravings caused her to stray away from the Candida elimination diet.

Soon after having me, she explained that she felt like she had been "zapped of energy" and started to feel badly again. She went back to her doctor and went back on Nystatin and following the Candida elimination diet.

During this time, she was experiencing secondary infertility and went on the drug Clomid to stimulate ovulation of the ovaries.

She had multiple miscarriages and the fertility doctor could not find anything wrong. My dad was also tested by a fertility doctor and his results came back normal.

Amid trying to figure out why she was so exhausted and why she couldn't get pregnant, life threw another curveball at her.

One morning, at age thirty-eight, she woke up and could not see out of her right eye.

All she could see were flashes of light.

She saw three different doctors for her eyes and received three separate diagnoses. The first was that it was just "bad luck." The other two were Histoplasmosis, an infection caused by breathing in fungus, and punctate inner choroidopathy, an inflammatory disease of the choroid and retina which can lead to vision loss.

After hearing conflicting diagnoses, she decided to take matters into her own hands.

Gail started seeing a naturopathic medical practitioner. Her new doctor recommended remedies that are dispensed in a liquid bottle. The liquids were made with a base of twenty-five percent grain alcohol and demineralized water. They were taken by mouth.

I vividly remember my mom using these sprays, and I thought they were disgusting! Her doctor also gave her special drops to put into water. We called it "dirty water" in our house.

In addition, she started to follow the advice given in a popular diet book at the time and ate primarily organic foods. She also continued to eat foods without yeast. Additionally, she cut out corn, wheat, lentils, tomatoes, peanuts, and chicken.

Unfortunately, even by eliminating these foods, she did not start to feel much better.

During this stage of my mother's life, she felt a lot of anxiety and stress. She was so fatigued with brain fog all of the time.

It became the new normal.

She often wondered what it would be like to get through a day without a nap—or two or three.

My mother was diagnosed with chronic fatigue and fibromyalgia, amalgam and heavy metal toxicity, and hormonal disturbances.

Even with the new diagnoses, she continued to follow the above protocol. She shopped in health food stores because, at this time, most grocery stores did not have organic foods. My mom followed this way of eating until she was about forty-four.

It had now been fifteen years of not knowing exactly what was going on with her body and what would heal her.

With frustrations of not getting better, my mom stopped following a specific diet or protocol.

She continued to be health conscious, but not as strict. She introduced unbleached flour and yeast back into her diet, making her own pizza, breads, and sticky buns. However, this new approach did not seem to show results either.

Looking for more answers, she started to go to an expert in "Total Body Modification, Koren Specific Technique, Contact Reflex Analysis and Microlight Therapy, a practitioner of Neuro Emotional Technique, and of Neural Organisational Technique."[192]

This new practitioner recommended a Sugar Elimination diet, which included eliminating any food that digests as a sugar in your body.

We did this diet together, and we lived on eggs, spelt bread, cheddar cheese, berries, broccoli, plain yogurt, and tons of salads.

I could only stick to this diet for three weeks.

I do not know how my mother did it for longer.

We also both took a lot of different supplements to support different organs in our body. My mom did see some progress from our alternative medicine practitioner's healing methods but wanted more support with her diet.

---

192 "About." Alternative Bliss, 2016.

At this point, my mom was fifty-two and still looking for a diet that made her feel energized.

She started to see an expert in regenerative medicine and began what was called a Bio-Metabolic Wellness Program.

She was instructed to eliminate all artificial sweeteners, gluten, dairy, soy, corn, foods with MSG, preservatives, tap water, and chewing gum. In addition, she was advised to cut out all processed foods, dead foods, toxic fats, and genetically modified foods.

On this cleanse, her diet was extremely strict. My mom primarily ate berries, vegetable soup, and apples. She also took some nutritional supplements, and was told to get fresh air and take a lot of walks.

During this time, I disliked coming home from college because home-cooked meals now consisted of cabbage soup— lots of cabbage soup.

She stuck to this diet for three months, and then continued following this new doctor's protocols for two years. She was diagnosed as prediabetic and knew she needed to get her blood sugar under control.

My mom lost ten pounds and felt better than she had in a long time.

However, at age fifty-four, she started to experience more brain fog, headaches, and exhaustion.

She thought that it may be due to the fact that she was working in a warehouse that sold cleaning compounds, exposing her to all kinds of toxins.

So, once again, my mom decided to follow her own diet. She continued to follow a gluten– and dairy-free diet and eat only organic foods.

Gail ate this way for about two years, until the summer of 2018. As I mentioned in the introduction, she then discovered the Medical Medium's dietary advice.

She heard about the Medical Medium through a friend and a podcast. After reading his book, *Medical Medium: Secrets Behind Chronic and Mystery Illness and How to Finally Heal*, she started following Anthony William's recommendations.

She began by incorporating celery juice into her morning routine. Then, she ordered a few of the herbs, vitamins, and minerals that were discussed in William's book. In addition, she got rid of all of the foods on his "no foods list."

This list was similar to the Bio-Metabolic Wellness Program. She did not eat gluten, dairy, soy, corn, pork, farm-raised fish, canola oil, egg, and foods with MSG or that were genetically modified.

Because Gail was seeing progress on this diet, she continued to research his diet and practice. She found a healing ambassador who was a student of the Medical Medium. Her healing ambassador recommended more supplements and that she start to eat more steamed and baked fruits and vegetables.

Gail started to eat more potatoes, sweet potatoes, brussels sprouts, peas, broccoli, leafy greens, apples, oranges, and dates.

On top of all of that, she began drinking the heavy metal detox smoothie once per day. These smoothies include fruits, greens, supplements, and coconut water.

My mom has done two of Anthony William's recommended cleanses, in addition to following his dietary advice.

After following this protocol for only six months, Gail's brain fog has been lifted, she has experienced less bloating and UTIs, has more youthful looking skin, gets minimal headaches, and is less fatigued than before. In addition, she believes her anxiety has decreased.

She is committed to following this protocol for as long as it continues to minimize all of these ailments.

She does not take any antibiotics or prescription drugs.

For the first time in almost thirty years, my mom feels like herself.

It's pretty incredible how the right foods can be used as medicine.

Finally, my mom added that this process may take one, two, or more years, but she is definitely seeing progress. She wakes up each day between 5:30 and 6:00 a.m., which was unheard of in years prior.

She "would roll out of bed, take me to school, and climb back in bed for another couple hours and still need a nap. Forget about exercise, and work was difficult to complete due to brain fog."

She had no focus.

Now, she has the energy to work out again like doing pilates, yoga, and cycling classes.

It's been almost a year of following the Medical Medium's guidelines, and her hope is that by this time next year, she will see even more positive results.

CHAPTER 16

RECOMMENDATIONS

———

Here are some products and brands I buy that make following the suggestions in this book a little bit easier.

VEGAN "DAIRY" PRODUCTS:

Culina
- Plain & Simple Yogurt

Follow Your Heart
- Dairy-Free Sour Cream

Miyoko's
- Sundried Tomato Garlic Cheese Wheel
- European Style Cultured Vegan Butter
- Fresh Vegan Mozzarella

- Plainly Classic Vegan Cream Cheese

Unfortunately, most of the other vegan dairy brands use cornstarch, canola oil, or other items on the Medical Medium "Do Not Eat List."

MEAT ALTERNATIVES:

Amy's
- Sonoma Veggie Burger

Hot Dang
- The Original Grain Burger

Again, many veggie burger brands seem perfect, and then you see that they use canola oil or corn as an ingredient.

GLUTEN SWAPS:

Food for Life
- Rice Almond Bread
- Brown Rice English Muffins

Siete
- Almond Flour Tortilla
- Grain Free Tortilla Chips

Simple Mills

- Sun-Dried Tomato and Basil Almond Flour Crackers
- Pizza Dough Almond Flour Mix
- Chocolate Muffin and Cake Almond Flour Mix
- Banana Muffin and Bread Almond Flour Mix

Tolerant Organic

- Red Lentil Penne
- Chickpea Pasta Rotini

Trader Joe's

- Organic Brown Rice & Quinoa Fusilli Pasta (Gluten-Free)

Thankfully, there are a lot of great gluten-free options available. The biggest ingredients to look out for when choosing gluten alternatives are eggs, canola oil, and cornstarch.

PRODUCE TO ALWAYS HAVE ON HAND:

- Organic frozen spinach
- Organic frozen kale
- Organic frozen broccoli
- Organic frozen riced cauliflower
- Organic frozen mushrooms
- Organic frozen wild blueberries
- Organic frozen mangoes

- Organic frozen pitaya (I like Pitaya Plus, Smoothie Pockets)
- Organic frozen mixed berries
- Organic frozen cranberries
- Organic bananas
- Organic granny smith apples
- Organic red delicious apples
- Organic avocado
- Organic cherry tomatoes
- Organic sweet potato
- Organic potato

I buy pretty much everything organic but be sure to review the EWG's "Clean Fifteen" and "Dirty Dozen" when you are making your choices!

PANTRY GO-TO ITEMS:

- Organic black beans
- Organic tomato paste
- Organic salsa (make sure it's corn and canola oil free)
- Organic pumpkin
- Organic raw & unfiltered honey
- Organic turmeric powder
- Organic Italian seasoning
- Organic fajita seasoning
- Organic chia seeds
- Organic flax seeds

- Organic cassava flour
- Organic tiger nut flour
- Organic arrowroot powder
- Organic coconut oil
- Organic avocado oil
- Namaste Gluten-free Organic Perfect Flour blend
- Premium Quality baking soda
- Trader Joe's Everything but the Bagel Sesame Seasoning Blend
- Himalayan pink salt

BEVERAGES:

365 Everyday Value
- Coconut Water

Native Forest
- Organic Unsweetened Coconut Milk

Uncle Matt's
- Organic Orange Juice

TEAS:

Matcha Love
- Japanese matcha + green tea tea bags

Spirit Healing Tea
- Liver Chai
- Lemon Balm
- Liver Detox

Traditional Medicinals
- Organic Dandelion Leaf & Root

Yogi
- Green Tea Super Antioxidant
- Vanilla Spice Perfect Energy

ADDITIONAL SNACKS:

Autumn's Gold:
- Grain Free Granola

Good Foods:
- Organic Avocado Mash

Jackson's Honest:
- Sea Salt Potato Chips
- Sweet Potato Chips

SUPPLEMENTS:

Vimergy:

- Wild Blueberry Dietary Supplement
- Barley Grass Juice Organic Powder
- Spirulina Dietary Supplement
- Dulse Sea Vegetable
- L-Lysine Dietary Supplement
- Ester-C Enhanced with Rosehips Dietary Supplement
- Zinc
- Liquid B12
- Lemon Balm
- Chaga Mushroom Extract Powder
- Melatonin Dietary Supplement

Nature's Answer:

- Cat's Claw

HARMONY:

- D-Mannose

Gaia Herbs:

- Ashwagandha Root

Mary Ruth's

- Daily Liquid Probiotic

CLEANING SUPPLIES:

Earth Friendly Products

- ECOS Window Cleaner, Lavender
- ECOS All Purpose Cleaner, Orange Plus
- ECOS Hypoallergenic Hand Soap, Lavender
- ECOS Shower Cleaner, Tea Tree
- ECOS 4X Hypoallergenic Laundry Detergent, Magnolia & Lilly

Seventh Generation

- Dishwasher Detergent Packs, Free & Clear
- Disinfecting Multi-Surface Cleaner, Lemongrass
- Disinfecting Multi-Surface Wipes, Lemongrass Citrus
- Dishwashing Liquid, Lavender Floral & Mint
- Free & Clear Laundry Detergent Pack
- Toilet Bowl Cleaner Natural Mint Scent

Thieves

- Dish Soap
- Household Cleaner
- Automatic Dishwasher Powder

COSMETICS AND SKIN CARE:

365 Everyday Value

- Maximum Moisture Body Lotion

Alba Botanica
- Coconut Oil Hawaiian Clear Spray SPF 50 Sunscreen
- Good & Clean Towelettes

Andalou Naturals
- Apricot Probiotic Cleansing Milk
- 1000 Roses Pearl Exfoliator
- Full Volume Lavender & Biotin Conditioner

Avalon Organics
- Smooth Shine Apple Cider Vinegar Shampoo

Dr. Bronner's
- Hand Soap

Dr. Hauschka
- Cleansing Cream

Josh Rosebrook
- Dry Shampoo
- Hair Spray

Living Libations
- Best Skin Ever - Seabuckthorn
- DewDab
- Happy Gum Drops
- Royal Rose CoQ10 Serum

Native
- Deodorant

Pacifica
- Tuscan Blood Orange Perfume

Periobrite
- Toothpaste

Tom's of Main
- Deodorant
- Toothpaste

Zuzu Luxe
- Dual Powder Foundation

I recommend using the Think Dirty App when looking at new cleaning and beauty products to try. The App tells you on a scale of zero to ten how dangerous the product might be.

HOUSEHOLD GOODIES:
- Essential oil diffuser
- Young Living essential oils
- Reed oil diffuser
- Berkey water filter (or Brita if your water tests pretty well)

OTHER:

Azalea
- Organic cotton tampons

COOKBOOKS TO USE:
- How Not to Die Cookbook by Michael Greger, M.D., FACLM
- Against All Grain by Danielle Walker
- Thug Kitchen Party Grub
- Medical Medium Blog
- Potatoes by Ash Foster

Obviously, if there are some items in recipes that you have decided to cut out, you can look up replacements for those ingredients that you can eat! I modify most recipes, but these books offer amazing starting points and ideas!

*Disclaimer: I am not a paid partner for any of these brands. Over the years, many of these brands are what my parents, Alexandra, and I have used because of the ingredients and positive ratings.

CHAPTER 17

THE JOURNEY CONTINUES

———

One night when Alexandra and I were walking through the dimly lit streets in Philadelphia, she asked me, "Have you ever heard of how the coal miners used to rely on canaries?"

I responded, "No, I have no idea what you are talking about."

She proceeded to tell me "when coal miners were working in a new area, they would put a canary in a cage. When the canary died because it ran out of usable oxygen, the coal miners knew it was time to get out of that area."

I thought to myself, okay, interesting story, but why did you bring up dead birds?

She explained that she thought of herself as a canary.

She got sick from eating certain foods, being surrounded by mold, and using chemical based products in her home and on her skin.

However, it seemed like no one around her was impacted, at least not on the surface.

Now after she completed extensive research on how food, water, and other products impact our health, she understood it may still be affecting her friends and family, just in less severe or apparent ways.

She believes she had to test out many different diets and products so other people do not have to suffer the way she did.

She is the canary.

Alexandra was able to turn her grueling ten-year healing journey into something positive. She wants to use her knowledge and experiences to help others avoid the pain that she has endured.

I truly believe Alexandra has been a canary for me, my mom, and Trish.

If I never ran into her at the Eagles game and saw how vibrant Alexandra was, I might not have looked into the Medical Medium and made changes to my diet.

But, as you know, Alexandra's diet and the remarkable results she has seen have not happened overnight.

Diet and lifestyle changes take time.

Alexandra needed to strictly follow Anthony William's protocol and remove toxins from every aspect of her life to truly heal.

My mother tried so many different diets until she found one that truly made her feel energized and healthy.

It took me almost a full year to eliminate or cut down on certain foods. The results I have seen from using research to guide my dietary choices have not happened immediately.

I believe Trish and I are still on the journey to truly heal. As of right now, neither of us are fully recovered.

I still get a pimple every once in a while or experience anxiety.

Trish's tumor is still not small enough to surgically remove.

However, both of us have seen results from the dietary and lifestyle changes we've made. Both of us are living much healthier lives than we were a year ago, and that is a huge start.

My immune system is stronger. I honestly cannot remember the last time I was sick with something as minor as a cold.

My digestive tract has improved, and I am actually absorbing the nutrients in my food.

I no longer wake up nauseous or light-headed.

I don't feel exhausted when I get home from work at 5:00 p.m. and feel the need to crawl into bed while the sun is still out.

I haven't gotten a UTI in months.

I've maintained a healthy weight that I feel confident about.

I never understood how much better my quality of life could be until I started making these dietary changes.

Trish's tumor has remained stable for the last year and a half. It has not grown since she was diagnosed with stage 4 cancer, and it has even shrunk a small amount. She is able to live a normal life full of work, exercise, and fun. Hopefully, as she continues to drink celery juice, eat a plant-based diet, exercise frequently, see her oncologist and alternative medicine practitioner, and enjoy time with her friends, she will see more positive results.

One year ago, Trish and I did not know most of the information in this book.

We did not know the importance that the liver and microbiome have on our health.

We did not know that plant-based diets have healed so many people.

We also did not know the dangers of many foods that we have considered healthy for our entire lives.

We couldn't change what we didn't know.

However, now that we have read the studies, we are much more conscious of what we put in our bodies and where our food comes from.

We are willing to redo our budgets to account for better quality food and products.

My hope is that you will use the information in this book to challenge what you have always thought of as "healthy."

I hope that you get the "Think Dirty" app on your phone and test the products you use on your skin and in your home.

I also hope that you use the "Dirty Dozen" as a guide when you are shopping for produce, and that you stop eating processed foods and meats.

Whatever changes you decide to make, whether it be to help a loved one who has been diagnosed with a chronic illness or cancer or to change your own diet, I hope you feel empowered to make choices now that you have information that is not typically discussed.

I want you to use the information in this book to join me and use food as medicine to give yourself the best quality of life that you can have.

ACKNOWLEDGMENTS

———

My dream of becoming an author began in high school. Any time that I would become "inspired" by a prominent experience or a story, I would start writing chapters of a book that did not exist. A few years later when I was teaching 7th grade writing, I told my students about my aspiration of becoming a published author. However, it was not until I watched important women in my life conquer their illnesses, and I had the direction from an amazing team, that my dream could become a reality.

Thank you first and foremost to my parents for supporting me through every step of the way. You have always encouraged me to follow my passion and believed in me when I doubted myself. Mom, thank you for being a model of health and vulnerability. This book would not have been possible without your knowledge and story. Dad, thank you for being the best editor and supporter.

Thank you Alexandra Currell and Trish Churchill for letting me be a part of your health journeys. Your strength and positivity is unmatched.

Thank you Megan Riley, Maria Mulheren, Vincanne Adams, Lauren Jokl, and Carolina Parra for letting me share parts of your experiences with diet.

You have all helped to shape my view of healthy eating.

In addition, thank you to everyone at New Degree Press, especially Eric Koester, Brian Bies, Stephanie McKibben, and Stephanie Gillett. Your expertise made this book into something that I could be proud of.

And thank you to everyone who: gave me their time for a personal interview, pre-ordered the eBook or paperback, helped spread the word about *We Can't Change What We Don't Know* to make publishing possible. I am sincerely grateful for all of your help.

Megan Riley, Gail Carney, Joe Carney, Hannah Carney, Kathleen Oldakowski, Sareena Sofat, Margaret McCaffery, Olivia Lundstrom, Sam Voge, Luke Self, Sydney Betts, Brian Coleman,

Maureen Coleman, Laura Jogani, Cindy Rebellon, Maria Mulheren, Doris Halley, Felice Stang, Taylor Barbato, Danielle Bannon, Zachary Berger, Gabrielle Love, Lauren Jokl, Ryan McCreary, Alayna Liska, Kimberlee Churchill, Albert Briones, Janelle Brown, Luis Caicedo, Liz O'Neill, Cat Wright, Shelby Welty, Delia Franchi, Trish Churchill, Paige Foley, Patricia Favoreel, Rachel Levenson, Hayley Brudish, Delaney Leonard, Tiffany Trankiem, Claire O'Neill, Carolina Parra, Kimberly Oldakowski, Bryce Andrukitis, Mike Holtz, Angela Zirino, Ashley Tant, Claire McDermott, Devon Townend, Melanie Discala, Mike McCaffery, Kristen Gianaras McCaffery, Kevin Davoli, Emma Santos, Meghan Moriarty, Benjamin Murray, Tori Levi, Katherine Camp, Justin Spencer, Judith Voge, Madeline Cowperthwaite, Sam Carney, Annie Procaccini, Olivia Loncki, Lisa Levi, Gabriel Busto, Maddy Scarff, Brooke Dutton, Brian Tran-Dac, Daniel Owens, Lisa VanSco, Ashley Brooks, Thomas Foley, Chrissy Strangie, Cordelia Tullous, Claire Carney, Joe Ambrose, Kristin Plansky, Maddy Gilligan, Mariel Geron, Rhonda Quinlan, Halie Welsh, Brittny Owens, Elise Harmon, Tyler Price, Andrew Shaw, Brendan O'Connor, Kathy Jokl, Rob Stone, Justin McCreary, Jackie Lovett, Mary Wright, Robin Smith, Amanda Hyman, Lauren Wilhelm, Lynn Fairweather, Jennifer Irey, Geneva DiPalma, Mark Schlickman, Kendall Maliszewski, Sherry Cetola, Carolina Garcia, Jennifer Fusco, Kasey Miller, Michael Keating, Wesley Robbins, Eric Koester, Lauren Cutler, Edward Carney, Tina Green, Brian O'Neill, Robbie Gilroy, Alex Kalter, Jonathon Cramer, Tim

McKinney, Giuliana Parisi, Nate Kong, Maddie Davis, Lynn Wong, Mike Carney, Abigail Lemmy, Sean Buckley. Colleen Blackney, Jennifer Halley, Melissa Chammas, Theresa McCullough, Sandra Corredor, Christine Patrick, Kaycee O'Neill, and Jules Feng.

WORKS REFERENCED

INTRODUCTION

Churchill, Trish. "Trish's Fight Against Thymoma." GoFundMe. GoFundMe, August 13, 2018.

Matej Mikulic, "Prescription Drug Expenditure U.S. 1960-2019," Statista (Statista 2019, August 9, 2019).

"Understanding the Epidemic | Drug Overdose | CDC Injury Center," Centers for Disease Control and Prevention (Centers for Disease Control and Prevention, National Center for Injury Prevention and Control, December 19, 2018).

CHAPTER 1

McDougall, John. "A Revelation: Your Health Is Not Determined by Heredity." Dr. McDougall's Health & Medical Center. John A. McDougall. Accessed October 9, 2019

Perro, Michelle, and Vincanne Adams. "Food-Focused Medicine for a Pharmaceutical-Heavy World." Essay. In What's Making Our Children Sick?: How Industrial Food Is Causing an Epidemic of Chronic Illness, and What Parents (and Doctors) Can Do about It, 31. White River Junction, VT: Chelsea Green Publishing, 2017.

Wark, Chris. "Doctor's Orders." Essay. In Chris Beat Cancer, 1st ed., 43–47. Carlsbad, CA: HAY HOUSE, INC, 2018.

Wark, Chris. "Heroic Doses." Essay. In Chris Beat Cancer, 1st ed., 126–28. Carlsbad, CA: HAY HOUSE, INC, 2018.

Wark, Chris. "Into the Jungle." Essay. In Chris Beat Cancer, 1st ed., 7–11. Carlsbad, CA: HAY HOUSE, INC, 2018.

William, Anthony. "Chapter 23 Acne." Essay. In Medical Medium Liver Rescue: Answers to Eczema, Psoriasis, Diabetes, Strep, Acne, Gout, Bloating, Gallstones, Adrenal Stress, Fatigue, Fatty Liver, Weight Issues, SIBO & Autoimmune Disease, 1st ed., 155–60. Carlsbad, CA: Hay House, Inc., 2018.

CHAPTER 2

Kshirsagar, Rijul, and Priscilla Vu. "The Pharmaceutical Industry's Role in U.S. Medical Education." in-Training. in-Training, April 5, 2016.

Li, William W. "Chapter 3 Microbiome." Essay. In Eat to Beat Disease: the New Science of How the Body Can Heal Itself, 35–43. New York, NY: Grand Central Life & Style, 2019.

Li, William W. "Chapter 3 Microbiome." Essay. In Eat to Beat Disease: the New Science of How the Body Can Heal Itself, 47. New York, NY: Grand Central Life & Style, 2019.

Li, William W. "Chapter 3 Microbiome." Essay. In Eat to Beat Disease: the New Science of How the Body Can Heal Itself, 48. New York, NY: Grand Central Life & Style, 2019.

"Medical Anthropology." Medical Anthropology | Department of Anthropology. Stanford University. Accessed October 9, 2019.

Perro, Michelle, and Vincanne Adams. "Food-Focused Medicine for a Pharmaceutical-Heavy World." Essay. In What's Making Our Children Sick?: How Industrial Food Is Causing an Epidemic of Chronic Illness, and What Parents (and Doctors) Can Do about It, 23. White River Junction, VT: Chelsea Green Publishing, 2017.

Perro, Michelle, and Vincanne Adams. "Food-Focused Medicine for a Pharmaceutical-Heavy World." Essay. In What's Making Our Children Sick?: How Industrial Food Is Causing an Epidemic of Chronic Illness, and What Parents (and Doctors) Can Do about It, 32. White River Junction, VT: Chelsea Green Publishing, 2017.

Perro, Michelle, and Vincanne Adams. "Leaky Gut: A Key to Understanding Pesticide Impact on Health" Essay. In What's Making Our Children Sick?: How Industrial Food Is Causing an Epidemic of Chronic Illness, and What Parents (and Doctors) Can Do about It, 81-92. White River Junction, VT: Chelsea Green Publishing, 2017.

Sarsina, Paolo Roberti Di, Luigi Ottaviani, and Joey Mella. "Tibetan Medicine: a Unique Heritage of Person-Centered Medicine." EPMA Journal 2, no. 4 (2011): 385–89.

What Causes Dysbiosis and How Is It Treated?" Healthline. Accessed October 9, 2019.

CHAPTER 3

D'Souza, Darryl. "The Liver." Essay. In Become Healthy or Extinct!, 6th ed., 33, 2019.

"Healthy Liver - 13 Tips on How to Have a Healthy Liver." American Liver Foundation, January 7, 2019.

William, Anthony. "Chapter 1 What Your Liver Does for You." Essay. In Medical Medium Liver Rescue: Answers to Eczema, Psoriasis, Diabetes, Strep, Acne, Gout, Bloating, Gallstones, Adrenal Stress, Fatigue, Fatty Liver, Weight Issues, SIBO & Autoimmune Disease, 1st ed., 5. Carlsbad, CA: Hay House, Inc., 2018.

William, Anthony. "Chapter 1 What Your Liver Does for You." Essay. In Medical Medium Liver Rescue: Answers to Eczema, Psoriasis, Diabetes, Strep, Acne, Gout, Bloating, Gallstones, Adrenal Stress, Fatigue, Fatty Liver, Weight Issues, SIBO & Autoimmune Disease, 1st ed., 6. Carlsbad, CA: Hay House, Inc., 2018.

William, Anthony. "Chapter 1 What Your Liver Does for You." Essay. In Medical Medium Liver Rescue: Answers to Eczema, Psoriasis, Diabetes, Strep, Acne, Gout, Bloating, Gallstones, Adrenal Stress, Fatigue, Fatty Liver, Weight Issues, SIBO & Autoimmune Disease, 1st ed., 8. Carlsbad, CA: Hay House, Inc., 2018.

Richer, Nicolette. "Detoxification." Essay. In Eat Real to Heal: Using Food as Medicine to Reverse Chronic Diseases from Diabetes, Arthritis to Cancer and More, 112–13. Coral Gables, FL: Mango, 2018.

CHAPTER 4

D'Souza, Darryl. "Causes of Chronic Illness and Disease" Essay. In *Become Healthy or Extinct!*, 6th ed., 24, 2019.

Li, William W. "Chapter 7 (Re)generate Your Health" Essay. In *Eat to Beat Disease: the New Science of How the Body Can Heal Itself*, 149. New York, NY: Grand Central Life & Style, 2019.

McDougall, John. "A Revelation: Your Health Is Not Determined by Heredity." Dr. McDougall's Health & Medical Center. John A. McDougall. Accessed October 9, 2019.

"Neuro Emotional Technique (NET)." Innovative Medicine. Accessed October 10, 2019.

Rosenbloom, Cara. "Not All Processed Foods Are Bad for You. How They're Made Matters." The Washington Post. WP Company, February 9, 2017.

Wolfram, Taylor. "Processed Foods Whats OK and What to Avoid." EatRight . Academy of Nutrition and Dietetics , February 11, 2019.

CHAPTER 5

"Clean Fifteen™ Conventional Produce with the Least Pesticides." EWG's 2019 Shopper's Guide to Pesticides in Produce | Clean Fifteen. Environmental Working Group, 2019.

D'Souza, Darryl. "Blending" Essay. In *Become Healthy or Extinct!*, 6th ed., 88, 2019.

"Dirty Dozen™ Fruits and Vegetables with the Most Pesticides." EWG's 2019 Shopper's Guide to Pesticides in Produce | Dirty Dozen. Environmental Working Group, 2019.

Hyman, Mark. "Vegetables." Essay. In Food: What the Heck Should I Eat?, 120. New York, NY: Little Brown & Co, 2018.

Weil, Andrew. "Are Frozen Vegetables Healthy? - Ask Dr. Weil." DrWeil, December 3, 2016.

CHAPTER 6

Perro, Michelle, and Vincanne Adams. "The Family Eating Modern Industrial Foods: Almost Everyone Is Sick." Essay. In *What's Making Our Children Sick?: How Industrial Food Is Causing an Epidemic of Chronic Illness, and What Parents (and Doctors) Can Do about It*, 57. White River Junction, VT: Chelsea Green Publishing, 2017.

Perro, Michelle, and Vincanne Adams. "The Family Eating Modern Industrial Foods: Almost Everyone Is Sick." Essay. In *What's Making Our Children Sick?: How Industrial Food Is Causing an Epidemic of Chronic Illness, and What Parents (and Doctors) Can Do about It*, 52-53. White River Junction, VT: Chelsea Green Publishing, 2017.

Perro, Michelle, and Vincanne Adams. "Food-Focused Medicine for a Pharmaceutical-Heavy World." Essay. In What's Making Our Children Sick?: How Industrial Food Is Causing an Epidemic of Chronic Illness, and What Parents (and Doctors) Can Do about It, 32. White River Junction, VT: Chelsea Green Publishing, 2017.

Richer, Nicolette. "Frequently Asked Questions about Food and Disease." Essay. In Eat Real to Heal: Using Food as Medicine to Reverse Chronic Diseases from Diabetes, Arthritis to Cancer and More, 48-49. Coral Gables, FL: Mango, 2018.

"Understanding Organic Foods." Unlock Food. Dietitians of Canada, December 3, 2018.

Wark, Chris. "Take Out the Trash" Essay. In Chris Beat Cancer, 1st ed., 166. Carlsbad, CA: HAY HOUSE, INC, 2018.

CHAPTER 7

Adams, Ashley. "If You Are Dairy-Free, Beware of These 11 Foods With Hidden Dairy." The Spruce Eats. The Spruce Eats, February 7, 2019.

D'Souza, Darryl. "Common Foods that ruin our Health." Essay. In Become Healthy or Extinct!, 6th ed., 120-125, 2019.

Hyman, Mark. "Milk and Dairy." Essay. In *Food: What the Heck Should I Eat?*, 76. New York, NY: Little Brown & Co, 2018

Hyman, Mark. "Milk and Dairy." Essay. In *Food: What the Heck Should I Eat?*, 77. New York, NY: Little Brown & Co, 2018.

Hyman, Mark. "Milk and Dairy." Essay. In *Food: What the Heck Should I Eat?*, 84-85. New York, NY: Little Brown & Co, 2018.

Hyman, Mark. "Milk and Dairy." Essay. In *Food: What the Heck Should I Eat?*, 88. New York, NY: Little Brown & Co, 2018.

Hyman, Mark. "Milk and Dairy." Essay. In *Food: What the Heck Should I Eat?*, 91. New York, NY: Little Brown & Co, 2018.

Johnson, Jon. "Dairy Alternatives: A Guide to the Best Dairy Substitutes." Medical News Today. MediLexicon International, October 22, 2018.

Li, William W. "Chapter 3 Microbiome." Essay. In *Eat to Beat Disease: the New Science of How the Body Can Heal Itself*, 45-47. New York, NY: Grand Central Life & Style, 2019.

Li, William W. "Chapter 8 Feed Your Inner Ecosystem." Essay. In *Eat to Beat Disease: the New Science of How the Body Can Heal Itself*, 167. New York, NY: Grand Central Life & Style, 2019.

McDougall, John. "A Revelation: Your Health Is Not Determined by Heredity." Dr. McDougall's Health & Medical Center. John A. McDougall. Accessed October 9, 2019.

McDougall, John. "Plant Foods Provide the Nutritional Building Blocks for Optimum Health." Dr. McDougall's Health & Medical Center. John A. McDougall. Accessed October 10, 2019.

Richer, Nicolette. "Eating Real." Essay. In Eat Real to Heal: Using Food as Medicine to Reverse Chronic Diseases from Diabetes, Arthritis to Cancer and More, 60-61. Coral Gables, FL: Mango, 2018.

Shabandeh, M. "Milk Retail Sales in the United States from 2005 to 2018 (in Billion Pounds)." Statista, June 26, 2019.

Wark, Chris. "Heroic Doses." Essay. In Chris Beat Cancer, 1st ed., 138-139. Carlsbad, CA: HAY HOUSE, INC, 2018.

Weil, Andrew. "Is Carrageenan Safe?: Food Additives: Andrew Weil, M.D." DrWeil, July 8, 2019.

CHAPTER 8

D'Souza, Darryl. "Common Foods that ruin our Health" Essay. In *Become Healthy or Extinct!*, 6th ed., 126-127, 2019.

D'Souza, Darryl. "The Right balance of Food." Essay. In *Become Healthy or Extinct!*, 6th ed., 55, 2019.

D'Souza, Darryl. "The Right balance of Food." Essay. In *Become Healthy or Extinct!*, 6th ed., 59, 2019.

"Ezekiel 4:9 Bread. and Better!" Food For Life. June 18, 2019.

Hyman, Mark. "Grains." Essay. In Food: What the Heck Should I Eat?, 186-187. New York, NY: Little Brown & Co, 2018.

Hyman, Mark. "Grains." Essay. In Food: What the Heck Should I Eat?, 187. New York, NY: Little Brown & Co, 2018.

Hyman, Mark. "Grains." Essay. In Food: What the Heck Should I Eat?, 193. New York, NY: Little Brown & Co, 2018.

Hyman, Mark. "Grains." Essay. In Food: What the Heck Should I Eat?, 201-202. New York, NY: Little Brown & Co, 2018.

Li, William W. "Chapter 8 Feed Your Inner Ecosystem." Essay. In Eat to Beat Disease: the New Science of How the Body Can Heal Itself, 174. New York, NY: Grand Central Life & Style, 2019.

Li, William W. "Chapter 12 Rethinking the Kitchen." Essay. In *Eat to Beat Disease: the New Science of How the Body Can Heal Itself*, 284. New York, NY: Grand Central Life & Style, 2019.

Richer, Nicolette. "Eating Real." Essay. In Eat Real to Heal: Using Food as Medicine to Reverse Chronic Diseases from Diabetes, Arthritis to Cancer and More, 59. Coral Gables, FL: Mango, 2018.

William, Anthony. "Chapter 23 Acne." Essay. In Medical Medium Liver Rescue: Answers to Eczema, Psoriasis, Diabetes, Strep, Acne, Gout, Bloating, Gallstones, Adrenal Stress, Fatigue, Fatty Liver, Weight Issues, SIBO & Autoimmune Disease, 1st ed., 159. Carlsbad, CA: Hay House, Inc., 2018.

CHAPTER 9

Churchill, Trish. "Trish's Fight Against Thymoma." GoFundMe. GoFundMe, August 7, 2019.

Hyman, Mark. "Meat." Essay. In Food: What the Heck Should I Eat?, 33-42. New York, NY: Little Brown & Co, 2018.

Hyman, Mark. "Meat." Essay. In Food: What the Heck Should I Eat?, 34. New York, NY: Little Brown & Co, 2018.

Hyman, Mark. "Meat." Essay. In Food: What the Heck Should I Eat?, 49. New York, NY: Little Brown & Co, 2018.

Li, William W. "Chapter 6 Starve Your Disease, Feed Your Health." Essay. In Eat to Beat Disease: the New Science of How the Body Can Heal Itself, 109. New York, NY: Grand Central Life & Style, 2019.

Li, William W. "Chapter 6 Starve Your Disease, Feed Your Health." Essay. In Eat to Beat Disease: the New Science of How the Body Can Heal Itself, 112. New York, NY: Grand Central Life & Style, 2019.

Li, William W. "Chapter 9 Direct Your Genetic Fate." Essay. In Eat to Beat Disease: the New Science of How the Body Can Heal Itself, 189-217. New York, NY: Grand Central Life & Style, 2019.

"Overview of Food Ingredients, Additives & Colors." U.S. Food and Drug Administration. FDA, April 2010.

Richer, Nicolette. "Eating Real." Essay. In *Eat Real to Heal: Using Food as Medicine to Reverse Chronic Diseases from Diabetes, Arthritis to Cancer and More*, 60-61. Coral Gables, FL: Mango, 2018.

"The Truth about Fats: the Good, the Bad, and the in-Between." Harvard Health Publishing. Harvard Medical School, August 13, 2018.

Wark, Chris. "Heroic Doses." Essay. In Chris Beat Cancer, 1st ed., 126. Carlsbad, CA: HAY HOUSE, INC, 2018.

Wark, Chris. "Heroic Doses." Essay. In Chris Beat Cancer, 1st ed., 127. Carlsbad, CA: HAY HOUSE, INC, 2018.

William, Anthony. "Truth About Protein." Medical Medium Blog. Anthony William, Inc. , September 7, 2018.

CHAPTER 10

D'Souza, Darryl. "Free Radicals and Antioxidants." Essay. In *Become Healthy or Extinct!*, 6th ed., 93, 2019.

D'Souza, Darryl. "Common Foods that ruin our Health." Essay. In *Become Healthy or Extinct!*, 6th ed., 132, 2019.

Flores, Vanessa. "Why You NEED to Eat Fat to Lose Weight." Strong4ByV. Strong4ByV, September 27, 2018.

Hyman, Mark. "Fats and Oils." Essay. In Food: What the Heck Should I Eat?, 147. New York, NY: Little Brown & Co, 2018.

Hyman, Mark. "Fats and Oils." Essay. In Food: What the Heck Should I Eat?, 161. New York, NY: Little Brown & Co, 2018.

Hyman, Mark. "Fats and Oils." Essay. In Food: What the Heck Should I Eat?, 162-163. New York, NY: Little Brown & Co, 2018.

Hyman, Mark. "Fats and Oils." Essay. In Food: What the Heck Should I Eat?, 169. New York, NY: Little Brown & Co, 2018.

Hyman, Mark. "Fats and Oils." Essay. In Food: What the Heck Should I Eat?, 169-170. New York, NY: Little Brown & Co, 2018.

Hyman, Mark. "Poultry and Eggs." Essay. In Food: What the Heck Should I Eat?, 69. New York, NY: Little Brown & Co, 2018.

Hyman, Mark. "Poultry and Eggs." Essay. In Food: What the Heck Should I Eat?, 69-70. New York, NY: Little Brown & Co, 2018.

Hyman, Mark. "Poultry and Eggs." Essay. In Food: What the Heck Should I Eat?, 72. New York, NY: Little Brown & Co, 2018.

Hyman, Mark. "Vegetables." Essay. In Food: What the Heck Should I Eat?, 126. New York, NY: Little Brown & Co, 2018.

Li, William W. "Chapter 6 Starve Your Disease, Feed Your Health." Essay. In Eat to Beat Disease: the New Science of How the Body Can Heal Itself, 118. New York, NY: Grand Central Life & Style, 2019.

McDougall, John. "Fat & Cholesterol: Primary Poisons." Dr. McDougall's Health Medical Center. John A. McDougall. Accessed October 10, 2019.

Richer, Nicolette. "Eating Real." Essay. In Eat Real to Heal: Using Food as Medicine to Reverse Chronic Diseases from Diabetes, Arthritis to Cancer and More, 58. Coral Gables, FL: Mango, 2018.

Richer, Nicolette. "Eating Real." Essay. In *Eat Real to Heal: Using Food as Medicine to Reverse Chronic Diseases from Diabetes, Arthritis to Cancer and More*, 60-61. Coral Gables, FL: Mango, 2018.

Wark, Chris. "Heroic Doses." Essay. In Chris Beat Cancer, 1st ed., 127. Carlsbad, CA: HAY HOUSE, INC, 2018.

William, Anthony. "Healing Acne." Medical Medium Blog. Anthony William, Inc. , June 22, 2017.

CHAPTER 11

D'Souza, Darryl. "Blending." Essay. In *Become Healthy or Extinct!*, 6th ed., 79, 2019.

D'Souza, Darryl. "Digestion." Essay. In *Become Healthy or Extinct!*, 6th ed., 100, 2019.

Richer, Nicolette. "Nutrient Absorption." Essay. In *Eat Real to Heal: Using Food as Medicine to Reverse Chronic Diseases from Diabetes, Arthritis to Cancer and More*, 111. Coral Gables, FL: Mango, 2018.

Wark, Chris. "Heroic Doses." Essay. In Chris Beat Cancer, 1st ed., 130. Carlsbad, CA: HAY HOUSE, INC, 2018.

William, Anthony. "Celery Juice." Medical Medium Blog. Anthony William, Inc., May 24, 2018.

William, Anthony. "Heavy Metal Detox Smoothie." Medical Medium Blog. Anthony William, Inc. , August 17, 2016.

CHAPTER 12

Gunnars, Kris. "10 Evidence-Based Health Benefits of Intermittent Fasting." Healthline, August 16, 2016.

Li, William W. "Chapter 11 The 5 x 5 x 5 Framework: Eating to Beat Disease." Essay. In Eat to Beat Disease: the New Science of How the Body Can Heal Itself, 274. New York, NY: Grand Central Life & Style, 2019.

Li, William W. "Chapter 11 The 5 x 5 x 5 Framework: Eating to Beat Disease." Essay. In Eat to Beat Disease: the New Science of How the Body Can Heal Itself, 275. New York, NY: Grand Central Life & Style, 2019.

Stage 3 Colon Cancer Survival Story. ChrisBeatCancer. YouTube, 2011.

Wark, Chris. "Take Out the Trash." Essay. In *Chris Beat Cancer*, 1st ed., 183. Carlsbad, CA: HAY HOUSE, INC, 2018.

Wark, Chris. "Take Out the Trash." Essay. In Chris Beat Cancer, 1st ed., 184. Carlsbad, CA: HAY HOUSE, INC, 2018.

Wark, Chris. "Take Out the Trash." Essay. In *Chris Beat Cancer*, 1st ed., 183-187. Carlsbad, CA: HAY HOUSE, INC, 2018.

CHAPTER 13

Hyman, Mark. "Beverages." Essay. In Food: What the Heck Should I Eat?, 246. New York, NY: Little Brown & Co, 2018.

Hyman, Mark. "Beverages." Essay. In Food: What the Heck Should I Eat?, 247. New York, NY: Little Brown & Co, 2018.

Hyman, Mark. "Beverages." Essay. In Food: What the Heck Should I Eat?, 252. New York, NY: Little Brown & Co, 2018.

Li, William W. "Chapter 6 Starve Your Disease, Feed Your Health." Essay. In Eat to Beat Disease: the New Science of How the Body Can Heal Itself, 115. New York, NY: Grand Central Life & Style, 2019.

Li, William W. "Chapter 6 Starve Your Disease, Feed Your Health." Essay. In Eat to Beat Disease: the New Science of How the Body Can Heal Itself, 116. New York, NY: Grand Central Life & Style, 2019.

Li, William W. "Chapter 8 Feed Your Inner Ecosystem." Essay. In Eat to Beat Disease: the New Science of How the Body Can Heal Itself, 182. New York, NY: Grand Central Life & Style, 2019.

Richer, Nicolette. "And What about Alcohol?." Essay. In *Eat Real to Heal: Using Food as Medicine to Reverse Chronic Diseases from Diabetes, Arthritis to Cancer and More*, 95. Coral Gables, FL: Mango, 2018.

Richer, Nicolette. "And What about Alcohol?." Essay. In *Eat Real to Heal: Using Food as Medicine to Reverse Chronic Diseases from Diabetes, Arthritis to Cancer and More*, 96. Coral Gables, FL: Mango, 2018.

CHAPTER 14

Deamer, Kacey. "Chromium-6 in Tap Water: Why the 'Erin Brockovich' Chemical Is Dangerous." LiveScience. Purch, September 22, 2016.

Li, William W. "Chapter 12 Rethinking the Kitchen." Essay. In Eat to Beat Disease: the New Science of How the Body Can Heal Itself, 279. New York, NY: Grand Central Life & Style, 2019.

Li, William W. "Chapter 12 Rethinking the Kitchen." Essay. In Eat to Beat Disease: the New Science of How the Body Can Heal Itself, 281. New York, NY: Grand Central Life & Style, 2019.

"Our Mission." Seventh Generation. Accessed October 10, 2019.

Richer, Nicolette. "All about Juicing." Essay. In Eat Real to Heal: Using Food as Medicine to Reverse Chronic Diseases from Diabetes, Arthritis to Cancer and More, 96. Coral Gables, FL: Mango, 2018.

Richer, Nicolette. "Cooking Techniques." Essay. In Eat Real to Heal: Using Food as Medicine to Reverse Chronic Diseases from Diabetes, Arthritis to Cancer and More, 73-74. Coral Gables, FL: Mango, 2018.

Richer, Nicolette. "Detoxifying the Home." Essay. In Eat Real to Heal: Using Food as Medicine to Reverse Chronic Diseases from Diabetes, Arthritis to Cancer and More, 144. Coral Gables, FL: Mango, 2018.

Richer, Nicolette. "Your Whole Health Plan." Essay. In Eat Real to Heal: Using Food as Medicine to Reverse Chronic Diseases from Diabetes, Arthritis to Cancer and More, 154. Coral Gables, FL: Mango, 2018.

Richer, Nicolette. "Your Whole Health Plan." Essay. In Eat Real to Heal: Using Food as Medicine to Reverse Chronic Diseases from Diabetes, Arthritis to Cancer and More, 155-156. Coral Gables, FL: Mango, 2018.

Richer, Nicolette. "Your Whole Health Plan." Essay. In Eat Real to Heal: Using Food as Medicine to Reverse Chronic Diseases from Diabetes, Arthritis to Cancer and More, 156. Coral Gables, FL: Mango, 2018.

Royte, Elizabeth. "We Know Plastic Is Harming Marine Life. What About Us?" National Geographic, May 16, 2018.

"Safer Choice." ECOS. Accessed October 10, 2019

"Thieves Products." Thieves Essential Oil Product Line | Thieves Oil Uses | Young Living Essential Oils. Accessed October 10, 2019.

Trimmer, Carol. "The Problem with Scented Candles & Your Health." Pure Living Space, December 8, 2017.

"What Is an Air Ionizer?: Air Ionizer Benefits." Air Oasis. Accessed October 10, 2019.

CHAPTER 15

"About." Alternative Bliss, 2016.

Axe, Josh. "Stop the Sugar Cravings and the Fuzzy Thinking!" Dr. Axe, January 25, 2019.

www.ingramcontent.com/pod-product-compliance
Lightning Source LLC
Chambersburg PA
CBHW071521180526
45171CB00002B/327